ALMOST A MOTHER

Love, Loss, and Finding Your People
When Your Baby Dies

Orange Hat Publishing
www.orangehatpublishing.com - Waukesha, WI

ALMOST A MOTHER

Love, Loss, and Finding Your People
When Your Baby Dies

Christy Wopat

Orange Hat Publishing
www.orangehatpublishing.com - Waukesha, WI

For information, please contact:

Orange Hat Publishing
www.orangehatpublishing.com
603 N Grand Ave., Waukesha, WI 53186

Edited by Christine Woods
Cover design by Kaeley Dunteman
Author photo by Luann Dibb

For my sweet Sophie and Aiden, who made me a mother.

And for Bree, and all my other baby loss moms, who gave me the strength to push on when I didn't think I could.

Early Praise for *Almost a Mother*

"Author Christy Wopat's book has all of the ingredients – humor, raw honesty, detail, and illuminating metaphor – to make it an engaging read. She transformed the horrendously horrible reality of having delivered twins (Sophie and Aiden) who both died within hours of birth into this gift for her readers. It is part memoir and part morality tale. It offers a reality check ("I am not crazy" or "I am crazy and that's ok") and catharsis to those with similar experiences and advice to those of us wondering how best to help them. It is rife with insights regarding grief, parenting, friendship, love, and identity."

- Dr. Ed de St. Aubin, Professor at Marquette University

"*Almost a Mother* speaks directly to the heart of all parents who have lost a baby. The raw experiences and emotions she shares are so relatable and heartwarming in the sense that you know you are not alone in your suffering and grief. Her strength in sharing her story will help other bereaved parents in their journey towards peace and hope."

- Rachel Redhouse, Director of Empty Cradle

"Pull up a comfy chair and a cup of tea, Christy Wopat's book is like a great conversation with a good friend. If you've had a stillbirth or early neonatal loss, you'll spend the whole time nodding in agreement. If you haven't, you'll be taken on an emotional journey through the resiliency of love. A mother's love is like no other, even when there's no one to 'mother.'"

- Amanda Ross-White, author of *Joy at the End of the Rainbow*,
Still Standing contributor

"Christy's writing is honest, raw, and genuine. Her book sheds light on what life is really like before, during, after the death of much-loved children. She lets you into her heart, mind, and soul, bearing even the darkest of moments to let you know you are not alone. There is no "right" or "wrong" in grief, only pain and love. This book beautifully dances in both the pain and the love."

- Kelly Cote, Evolve Counseling, LLC

"I LOVED *Almost A Mother*! Christy Wopat writes about grief and loss as only another mama who has lost her precious babies can. Her book is so relatable, funny, poignant, and comforting. I found myself nodding along through *Almost A Mother*, thinking, "yes, me too," as I read Christy's accounts of the crazy, wrong things people say when you're grieving ("they would have been serial killers"? Really?!), the sudden appearance of babies and twins everywhere, and the feelings of invisibility a loss mother feels as friends and family think you ought to be "moving on," or "getting over it." I felt like I had just made a new baby loss mom friend while reading it!

I highly recommend *Almost A Mother* to anyone who has lost a baby or babies, and especially to friends or loved ones seeking to understand what it's like to grieve the loss of a child at any age or gestation. Christy's book gives readers insight into the depths of sadness, the breadth of infinite love, and even the surprising moments of wry, (sometimes understandably dark!) humor that bereaved parents experience after the loss of a baby. It is a beautiful, heartfelt tribute to her twins, Sophie and Aiden, and to the capacity of the human heart to heal and find joy even after a painful loss."

- Robynne Knight, Founder of The Zoë Project,
Still Standing contributor

"Christy has managed to capture what my heart has felt for so many years. There are some instances in life that happen after you lose a child that laughter is the only thing that keeps you sane. She has magically put into words a balance that defines her love for her children and at the same time gives the reader hope that there can be joy again. If you have lost a child- this book can bring you hope once again."

- Megan Skaggs, Division Coordinator, Project Sweet Peas

"*Almost a Mother: Love, Loss, and Finding Your People When Your Baby Dies* is a moving, truthful memoir told with sharp wit and compassionate honesty. It is a story of grief that uncovers layers of feeling, and shows, through personal testimony how trauma can turn into bitterness, shame, jealousy, and rage. How others (who cannot be in your shoes) say hurtful things, though they don't mean to be unkind.

Life teaches everyone survival lessons, and protecting ourselves from the pain of others is human. Christy Wopat understands this, as she understands her own rage and frustration, her desire for time out while she recovers from a terrifying attachment-loss.

Erasure of identity, added to loss, brings bitterness and rage, landing life's journey, expected to be normal, into hazardous mountains of anguish, an anguish that must be understood to give birth to a future. In the end, this is a book about triumph, a triumph that would not have been possible if this teacher (and bereaved mother) had not chosen to discard unhelpful therapies and reach out to people online who have gone through what she went through. She had to find her people and build bridges to come out of her private darkness.

I read Christy's memoir as a sort of pilgrim's progress. Despite its hard-edged, concrete realism, *Almost a Mother* reads like an arduous sea-voyage that reaches an island of peace emblematized in reliable friendship, stronger family ties, and a marriage, that, based on love and loyalty, becomes stronger. Concomitantly, Christy's work as a teacher is now more meaningful to her.

The journey towards motherhood, even an arduous one, need not derail a woman's work. *Almost a Mother* is a faithful record of 21st-century female heroism that transcends conventional clichés. It is an inspiring book that everyone ought to read."

- Dr. Lalita Pandit Hogan, Professor of English at UW-La Crosse

TABLE OF CONTENTS

Dear Reader,

If you are reading this, there's a likelihood that you or someone close to you has just lost a baby. First, please know that there are no real words for the pain that you are feeling. This grief is like no other, and your grief is like no other. Next, please know that *Almost a Mother* is not at all what I think about myself. I know I will always be a mother to my babies even though they are not here.

I wrote this book because after my infant twins died, I couldn't find anything on the shelves at the bookstore that was actually honest. I found books about grief, sure. Books written by psychologists on the stages of grief and books that assured me that I would find my answers in prayer. This isn't meant to replace those. Those books are necessary, but in the raw, emotional weeks and months after losing my twins, what I wanted to know more than anything was that I was not crazy.

I wanted to know that the thoughts and feelings I was having didn't mean that I was the crazy lady on the made-for-TV movie who lost a baby and then went around stabbing people. I needed to know that I was not alone.

I wanted to know that my rage against the pregnant lady checking out at the grocery store didn't mean that I was suddenly a terrible person. That I was going to be okay.

In the pages of this book, you may disagree with thoughts or feelings that I have about grief. I tried very hard to make it known that in no way do I think that my thoughts are the only "right" ones. On the contrary—I know that everyone has their own journey. I just need to share mine in the hopes that someone can connect to my story and maybe find some peace.

What I hope more than anything is that you find some solace in knowing that you are not alone. That the hard work you are up against will be worth it. That someday the edges of the pain will eventually dull and, with any luck, the painful memories will turn into loving thoughts about the precious babies we lost.

I'm not going to lie—it might be a while. In the meantime, hang in there. Find your people, and lean on them. You've got this.

All my love,
Christy Wopat

CHAPTER 1 - SOMETHING CATASTROPHIC

From: Christy@email.com
Subject: Guess WHAT!?
Date: January 16, 2009
To: sarita127@email.com, readwritedream@email.com, dancing_
queen@email.com, pianogirl@email.com

Hello, everyone! It's Christy. You are NOT going to believe this . . .
I am pregnant with TWINS! Julia, twins, just like you! OMG! Do you
have any tips? I ordered two books already, but I could use some real-
life stories. (Like how do you open your car door when you're holding
two babies? I mean, for real!)

Brian is already worried about how much they're going to cost. His
brain skipped right to high school and wondered how much prom is
going to cost, LOL. He just told me we have to cut cable. I thought
maybe we could wait until high school.

I feel huge already, and I'm totally sick all the time. BARF, yo! My
mom got me these motion sickness bands to put around your wrists and
they do nothing.

The twins are due on August 7th, but the doctors already told me
that twins usually come early, so I'm starting to get ready already. Two
cribs, you guys!

Let's get together before I have TWO babies and will never be able
to sleep again. Miss you!

Smooches!!

Christy*

*Spelling, grammar, and punctuation left uncorrected in emails and text messages.

"Baby. Babe. Something is wrong. Oh my God. Oh my God! Something is wrong!" I rolled myself out of bed and onto the floor, and as I did, I felt a gush of fluid rush down my leg. I couldn't focus. I felt dizzy. *Liquid. Warm fluid. Did I pee myself? It had to be my water breaking. But that couldn't be right. At only twenty-one weeks pregnant, your water isn't supposed to break. Right?*

Brian jumped out of bed and ran over to me asking, "What is it? What's going on? What happened?" I explained what I felt, and he looked at me with wild eyes. "Okay, Okay. What do we do?"

I knew I should stay calm, but I couldn't figure out how to do it. The water was literally gushing down my legs with every step I took. "We have to go. We have to go to the hospital. Something is seriously wrong. This is not okay. It's not okay, so we have to go."

"Go where? Where do we have to go?" He sounded so far away from me.

"The hospital," I whispered. "Take me to the hospital."

"Okay. Okay. Hospital." He looked around and up at the clock, which read 9:40. The streetlights had just come on that night, and one was shining through the window. "Come on, Louis, in your bed," he said in a calm voice. The puppy stood up slowly. His tags jingled as he stretched and yawned then jumped down from the bed and sauntered toward the door. I moved slowly and carefully down the hall, holding onto the railing with one hand and resting the other under my pregnant belly. There was no way this was happening. My chest felt like someone was stepping on it, and I had to remind myself to take breaths.

As we reached the top of the staircase, I looked at my husband. "Babe, I need new pants and a towel, please." I went down the stairs and helped the dog get into his kennel. I didn't know what else to do, so I stepped out of my dripping wet clothes right there, next to the door, and left them in a pile at my feet. "I'll get that later," I said to no one, as if it mattered.

I walked into the garage and put the towel down on the front seat of the car. How funny that I would care at all about getting my seat wet when my life was crumbling down around me. My replacement pants were already soaked through. As I got into the car, I accidentally pushed on my stomach. It felt . . . soft. I was losing my breath. My heart was pounding.

My poor, sweet husband didn't understand. "It's going to be okay, babe. It's going to be fine. The doctors will fix it. Don't worry, it'll be fine."

I just stared out of the window at the darkness in the sky. *My stomach is soft*, I thought. *They can't fix that.* Our car kept speeding toward the hospital, but in my mind time was standing still, and we were going nowhere. I was frozen; I could barely breathe. I was afraid to move, afraid to touch my stomach again and find out that it was still soft. That would make what was happening actually real, and I needed it *not* to be real.

As we neared the hospital, I started to moan. Sounds escaped from my lips that were not actual words, just pain. It was the sound of pain. "Babe, this is not okay. We are not going to be okay. This is the end. This is the end. It's all over."

It's funny because I was saying that, but I didn't really know what was happening or what was over or not over. I had never heard of this happening. In the movies, when the woman's water breaks, everyone gets super excited, and people cheer and rush into action. When someone's water breaks, it means the baby is coming. And these babies should not have been coming. It was March, and they were not supposed to arrive until July. I couldn't understand. I couldn't wrap my brain around it.

Brian skidded into a parking spot and ran over to my side of the car. He threw open my door and put his arm around me as he helped me out. As we stepped into the cold air, I made a point to turn my face away from his. I couldn't let him see what I already knew because it would break him. We walked into the emergency room and up to the counter to talk to a triage nurse. "Hello. Can I help you?" she asked, without looking up from her computer.

"My, uh, my water just broke," I answered.

She looked at me. "Oh, congratulations! Great! We'll get you into a wheelchair and get you up to labor and delivery. Did you call and tell them you were on your way?"

I looked at the floor as someone helped me into a wheelchair. "I'm twenty-one weeks and three days pregnant."

All of a sudden, everyone around me moved a little faster, although at the same time everything seemed to stop. There were whispers and conversations. The air became thick with worry. Someone pushed me toward an elevator.

"Stop! No! Don't take her in there. We need a doctor to take her in the elevator," yelled the triage nurse.

That seemed idiotic to me. My face flushed with anger. *Why would they need a doctor to take someone up in the elevator?* I said, "I don't need a doctor to go in the elevator; that's ridiculous. You just take me. Or I'll take the stairs."

"Ma'am," she said. "You could go into labor any minute now. You need to stay in a wheelchair, but you also need a doctor, you know, in case something would happen in the elevator. We'll have someone here in just a minute."

Labor. In labor? But I hadn't taken my labor and delivery class. I didn't have my playlist or my labor gown or my slippers. I hadn't even packed my hospital bag yet. I couldn't go into labor. Not now. Next to me, Brian turned as white as a sheet. His hand gripped mine so hard his knuckles turned white.

Moments later, a man came around the corner and introduced himself. "I'll be taking you upstairs to labor and delivery. We'll get you into a room to see what we can find out. In many cases, women think their water broke, but they've actually just urinated on themselves. Please try to relax."

A nurse who was walking behind us added, "You probably just peed yourself. And if your water did break, we'll just keep you here on the floor until you're ready to have those babies. You might get sick of us after a few weeks, but we've made it work before."

Relief washed over me. Maybe I *had* just urinated on myself! That could totally be it. As we traveled up in the elevator, I felt calmer. Maybe I was wrong, and this wasn't as bad as I thought it was. I could stay in the hospital until the babies were fully ready to be born. I had heard of a friend who needed to be on bedrest during her pregnancy, and everything turned out fine for her and her babies. Bedrest didn't sound that bad, did it?

As soon as we were upstairs, I was put in a hospital gown and in a bed. An ultrasound machine was brought over, and there was an instant barrage of questions.

"About how much fluid would you say it was?"

"Are you feeling any pain or cramps?"

"Are you feeling the babies kick or move?"

"When was the last time you ate?"

I answered the questions as best I could, but I was focused on the technician next to me who was alternating between rubbing the cold blue jelly on my stomach and typing things into the computer. I watched her type, "Stomach appears to be soft." There it was again. My hand moved to my belly and pushed. Soft.

Several minutes and questions later, a new doctor appeared and introduced himself as Dr. Sanders, the perinatologist. I recognized him right away as the doctor who was assigned to high-risk pregnancy cases. We had been in his office once. "In the United States, eleven percent of twins are born weighing less than 3 pounds," he had told us. We were both angry when we left. I mean, the nerve of him!

Now he stood before us again, ready to deliver even more frightening news. "Christine," he began, "it is my opinion that the amniotic sac surrounding Baby A has broken. The ultrasound is showing us that your amniotic fluid is quite low. We are going to do one more test with litmus paper to make sure that it is amniotic fluid that is leaking and not urine, but you and your husband should be prepared to go into labor and deliver these babies within the next twelve hours."

Darkness swirled around me and rushed in, consuming my thoughts. Deliver the babies. Twelve hours. Baby A. Baby A was my girl. My little girl.

The test with the litmus paper was excruciatingly painful, but it barely dulled the sharp edge of the pain that was already there. The litmus paper test gave us the results right away. It made a "fern" shape; it was amniotic fluid.

"I'm sorry, Christine. We need to move you to a different delivery room that is close to the ER in case you need a C-section. Are you feeling any labor pains? Any cramping? Someone will be in soon to insert an IV in case we need it. Do you need to call anyone?"

I heard Brian call his mom while someone asked me even more questions. He sounded so small and so scared, almost like a little boy. I listened while he asked her to get the dog and bring it to her house, and he told her we were in the hospital, but he didn't say why. Suddenly, he was crying on the phone, which almost killed me. He knew, finally, that this was bad. That things were *not* going to be okay.

Once we were in the new room, they set up something to monitor my contractions. Except I wasn't having any contractions. This puzzled the doctors a little, but they kept coming back to check the paper that the machine spit out. A nurse would come in every ten minutes, and after seeing the paper, he would shrug, shake his head, and leave.

As I laid there, I thought about the names we had just chosen for our babies. "Aiden James" for our boy. "James" after Brian's dad, who had died from lung cancer just months before. "Sophie Mae" for our little girl. "Mae" for my grandma, my best friend. My sweet babies.

My daydreaming was interrupted by someone at our door. He was wheeling in another hospital bed. "We thought we'd bring this in for your husband," he said. He pushed it right up next to my bed. Brian climbed in and grabbed my hand.

We stayed in that same position, without moving, until morning.

***

I didn't sleep at all that night. People were in and out, sure, but mostly my mind just kept going over the recent events. I tried to figure out what I had done wrong to make this happen. *I knew I shouldn't have moved those tables all by myself for the potluck at school. I knew I shouldn't have been working out at the gym when even walking gave me side pains.* Mostly, though, I knew something had been wrong the week before when I had gone to the bathroom and seen some thick jelly-like substance on the toilet paper. I had called both of my doctors' offices, and they both said not to worry. *Could that have been a sign?*

What was it? I should've made myself go in for a checkup. I shouldn't have listened when they said not to worry.

During the early hours of the morning, I found my cell phone and dialed my mom.

"Mama?" I whispered, not wanting to alert Brian.

"What is it? What's wrong?" She sounded so sleepy, so disoriented.

"Mama." The sobs came easily now. Brian shifted beside me. "We're in the hospital. Me and the babies. It's really bad. So bad."

That woke her up. "What happened? What do you mean it's bad?"

My mouth had trouble forming the words. I thought about her other daughter. Her stillbirth. How we had talked about it just the week before.

"Please come, Mama. Please come right now." I shook as I hung up the phone. Brian moved closer to me and grabbed my hand again.

By about 10:00 the next morning, the doctor stood next to my hospital bed, puzzled. He had told me all night that I would be going into labor. I had read enough to know that once your water broke, you had to be careful of infection because there was nothing there anymore to protect you or the baby from the outside world. But then the nurse had said, "We'll just keep you on the labor and delivery floor." I chose to focus on that and play it over and over in my head. By noon that day, my mom arrived, and with the sunlight and no sign of labor, I allowed a little ray of hope to creep into my heart.

I was moved into a regular room in the postpartum part of the wing, although I was given an emergency labor kit to keep in my room because, as I was reminded, "Early labor like this can go really, really quickly." I could hear babies crying all day and all night long, which was upsetting to say the least. Occasionally I would wake up disoriented, and it would seem like the crying baby was in my room. This was followed every time by a harsh snap back to reality.

I asked my mom to bring me a computer so we could look up some of the terms the doctor was using. He told us right away that we had a case of PPROM, or preterm premature rupture of membranes. It sounded, like everything else, terrifying. A quick search told me we were in a lot of trouble. The statistics looked awful. Something like three percent of all pregnancies were inflicted with this condition, and the rate of morbidity was very high. Another alarming article informed us that not only were the babies at risk due to infection, but so, too, was the mother.

Digging deeper, I found a website that listed first-hand accounts from thousands of mothers who had experienced PPROM. My mouse lingered over the site, not sure where to click. It was divided into two sections: "Success Stories" and "Stories about Loss." I clicked "Success Stories."

"I was twenty-one weeks pregnant when I stood up from my chair and my water broke. I stayed in the hospital for six weeks with antibiotics, and my baby boy was born at twenty-seven weeks. He has some learning disabilities now as a seven-year-old, but overall he is a happy, healthy little boy."

My heart was pounding as I clicked next on a loss story.

"After my twenty-week ultrasound, I was so excited to meet my baby. The next week I lost my mucus plug. I called the doctor, scared, and the nurse told me not to worry. Two days later my water broke and my baby boy, Joseph, was born. I held him, and then I buried him."

The anger and fear rose up inside of me, immediately choking the joy that the success story had created. *My babies were probably going to die.* I knew it. I had known it. Now, I had seen it.

I made a valiant effort, but I couldn't stay away from that website. I devoured story after story, all day long, until I had read them all. Depending on the minute, I decided my babies would survive, or they would die. I didn't tell Brian. I didn't tell my mom. I told no one about this website.

I cried without stopping, and I was told to calm down. "Be confident for the babies," I was told. I needed to be "strong" for the babies. I needed to let go of my stress because it was "dangerous" for my pregnancy. A family member told me, as she walked out the door, that I needed to be strong because everyone was "counting on me to save these babies."

As if it were up to me.

The second morning our doctor came in and told us that we were not out of the woods by any means because the majority of these cases involved labor beginning almost instantly, I would be staying in the hospital indefinitely, and his nurse would be in to speak with us about some options.

Right away I was concerned. I had read a few stories on the PPROM website about instances when physicians had forced mothers to terminate their pregnancies and go into labor since the moms were in danger of infection, and the chance of survival for the babies was so low. If those were my options, I didn't want to hear them.

The perinatologist's nurse, a petite redhead with short, spiky hair, came in later and told my mom to leave the room. I nodded approval at my mom as she walked out, muttering something about coffee. The nurse sat down in a chair and pulled it to the corner of my bed. "My name is Linda," she started, "and here is my business card. I'm here for whatever you need. What you need right now, in my opinion, is to hear the truth. We don't know what is going to happen here, but you have yourselves in a pretty bad situation. And I owe it to you to be honest with you. You need to start thinking about funeral arrangements. I've brought some brochures for you to look at when you're ready. But don't delay because we don't know how much time you have. I hope you won't have to use any of this, but you need to look at it. I'm sorry. Are there any questions you have right away?"

We stared at the floor, silent. I could feel Brian's gaze burning into me, but I couldn't look. I turned the brochures over in my hand. "Cremation is an option, even for very small babies. We recommend calling funeral homes to find out the options in your preferred area."

I glanced down at a list of phone numbers of area funeral homes. On the cover was a smiling man, head tilted in sympathy, looking at two parents.

That night we sat in silence and stared at the clock to see it turn 9:41. Brian and I hugged as tears streamed down our faces. We'd gotten past the scariest part, according to the doctors at least—it had been twenty-four hours since my water broke, and there were still no signs of labor. I was getting very strong antibiotics through my IV, and on top of extreme bouts of nausea from that, I was dizzy from lack of sleep and the terror and stress I felt. But celebrate we did, anyway, because we had made it through the first step.

"Maybe . . . maybe it's going to be okay," I remember saying to Brian. He had always seemed so sure it would be okay, while I was sure it would be over. "Do you think we should start hoping?"

"Of course we should start hoping. Little Baby A and Baby B are going to be tormenting us for the rest of our lives! We've got this." He enveloped me in a hug. "We've got this."

Things were looking up—we had made it to the twenty-four hour mark, and I wasn't even having a contraction. What's more, I was really starting to feel the babies kick! That had to be a great sign. My girl, Sophie, would kick over and over all night long, and it felt like her brother would echo her movements.

***

The first time Brian wanted to go home to get some clothes and take a shower, I had the first real panic attack of my life. My chest felt as though it was in a vice, my heart suddenly and erratically pounding like a freight train. I just knew that as soon as he left, I would go into labor, and I'd have to do it all by myself.

I sat on the edge of the bed while tears streamed down my face, and I rubbed my belly with my hand. My words streamed out with big breaks in between so I could catch my breath. "I . . . just . . . please . . . don't . . . leave me here."

On some level I knew I was being irrational, but I imagined him getting in a car accident on the way home. In fact, this would be the beginning of many years of anxiety about my husband dying. I imagined he would leave the hospital, and I would die while delivering the babies without him. I imagined having to make any myriad of decisions, and it made me sick to my stomach. At this point, even choosing what to eat for dinner felt like something I just couldn't decide by myself.

Eventually, he found a friend to "babysit" me.

The next few days passed at a snail's pace. Brian screened phone calls for me. My mom had gone home, saying, "Honey, I need to go to work, but I can come right back if you need me—I promise." I think she just couldn't handle being there, seeing the pain so close and so real, remembering her own loss. My mother-in-law came to visit, but we didn't know what to say. No one else in our family said much beyond, "It'll be fine! Praying for you!" It was up to the two of us to deal with reality, it seemed.

One day there was a knock at my door, and it was a pizza delivery man. I sort of froze for a minute. "Are you Christy? This is a delivery for you." Taking the box, I set it on my bed. I opened it, and there was a pizza with the pepperonis shaped into a smiley face. Black marker scrawled on the inside said, "Love: Danny, Sarah, and Julia." My crazy, lovable best friends from college had delivered us a pizza. Brian looked over my shoulder to view the masterpiece. The laughter came slowly, bubbling up to the top. We stood there, bellies bouncing with laughter, feeling a bit nuts. It felt so good, so incredible, to have this insane feeling of joy brought on by such a small thing.

After seven days in the hospital and still no change, everyone was puzzled. One morning the perinatologist came in for his morning rounds to find me knitting a scarf. He sighed, "Well, you should know that I'm thinking about sending you home. You've finished your course of antibiotics, and we can't give you any more right now lest you become resistant to them. You're too early for a steroid shot, so we can't do that. I'm thinking we should get you out of here and into your own bed. You can stay at home until you go into labor, but you'll have to come back for checkups."

I let out a whimper, tears coming so easily and so forcefully. The doctor sighed again, his annoyance with me obvious. "Look, you really will be much happier at home." I was frozen with fear. Leaving that hospital meant leaving safety. Every minute of every day felt like it would be the last. I had read stories about complications with the umbilical cord after it moved around too much without fluid in the amniotic sac. I was afraid I would go into labor and deliver so quickly, like they had told me. I was terrified of being alone.

"I'm not ready to go home," I protested. "If I go home, they are going to die. We might all die."

Home we went. They didn't give us a choice. They said I was lying in a hospital bed when I could be lying in bed at home, where I would be "comfortable." We were discharged later that afternoon and sent home with an appointment set up for a few days later. As we left, the nurse said, "Okay, we'll see you guys next week . . . unless something catastrophic happens in the meantime."

"Got it," I said. "Catastrophic."

CHAPTER 2 - HEROIC MEASURES

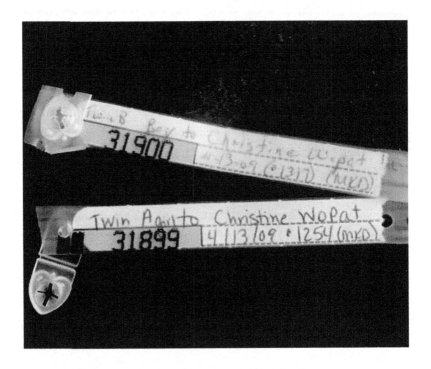

Brian held my hand as we walked through the doorway of our house. I walked ever so slowly and carefully, as if something might erupt inside of me if I moved too quickly, and it would all be over. I set my things down, and my dog, Louis, ran over to me and jumped up, his tail wagging with excitement.

"Get DOWN!" Brian yelled, his tone angry and resentful, and he reached down and swatted the dog away.

"It's okay. He's fine," I assured him, but he pulled him away anyway and put him in his kennel. As if an afterthought, a pang of guilt, he grabbed a dog treat and threw it into the cage through the bars.

The stairs stood in front of me, taunting me. I was weak and tired and really unsure about how I was going to complete the gargantuan task of going up. My orders were to be on complete bedrest, but I needed to get to the bed somehow.

I lifted my leg up on the first step, put a bit of weight on my foot, and I immediately felt a gush between my legs. I whimpered as I began to hurry up the stairs. I needed it over with. I walked right past the twins' nursery, grateful that the door was pulled shut. I collapsed on the bed in my room, tears streaming down my face. I squeezed my eyes shut as a flashback began. I could hear the "pop" sound as my water broke, and I tried to think of something else.

Brian came in the door just then, struggling with a mini-fridge. "I've got this to put next to your bed, so you can always have things to drink or eat," he said. "I got this from school, and I'll get it filled up for you. My mom will be here, but she wants to let you rest, so only call her if you need her."

I watched, helplessly, as he made trip after trip with water, soda, applesauce, fruit, cheese. I realized I didn't even know who had purchased any of this or when. He plopped down an enormous mug of ice water on the makeshift table next to my bed. "Remember to drink!" he declared. "I'm going to get some things done around the house. Yell if you need me."

"Lucky you," I muttered under my breath. There I was, confined to that room, the room with all of the flashbacks, where I could do nothing except watch bad television and try not to think about it. I was jealous that he could move around, stay busy, go to work to distract himself.

I rolled over to try to grab the TV remote, and as I did I felt another little gush of fluid. To feel the fluid leaking from me was excruciatingly frightening. Every time I got up to use the bathroom, every time I coughed or sneezed, and sometimes when I wasn't even moving, I could feel the fluid seeping out. Sometimes just a little, other times much more. I was drinking more than a gallon of water a day to try to combat the leaking, and it was all just coming right back out of me. The very thing that was necessary to keep my babies alive and help their lungs develop was slipping right out, and I could do nothing to stop it.

There is a feeling that I cannot quite describe when you are looking death in the eyes. It's like you know it's coming, and you know you can't stop it, but accepting it feels like giving up. I wanted so badly to believe that we were all going to be okay, but I knew that was a lie. On the other hand, I knew I couldn't spend my days waiting, sure that death would arrive.

A man I taught with at the middle school sent me an email while I was on bedrest. He explained that he believed in the power of the universe, and that there was a secret to getting anything you wanted. The steps were this: (1) identify what you don't want; (2) get clear about what you do want; (3) feel what it would be like to have those things; and (4) allow the universe to bring those things to you. I remember reading it over and over again, wondering, perhaps even hoping, *could it be that simple?*

I thought, *sure, you want that job, go get it. Believe in yourself! You want to lose weight? Picturing yourself thin might help make that happen.* That made enough sense to me. But, could I really *will* the universe into letting my babies live?

Those sort of things really just seemed to trivialize what was happening, in my opinion. Just months before, we had watched my father-in-law die an excruciatingly painful death from lung cancer. For the first time in my life, I had truly come to understand how little control we actually have over life and death—and I felt like I was being reminded of it all over again.

I remembered a time when Brian and I had been driving home in an ice storm. We were driving so slowly, so carefully, but as we finally pulled into the parking lot of our apartment, we hit a patch of ice. When the tires hit that patch of ice, there was not a damn thing either of us could do to stop the inevitable. As we turned and twisted, I realized that we were heading straight for a garage door, and we crashed through it even though we weren't going more than a mile or two an hour. Basically, it's that feeling when you can see the crash coming, but you're totally screwed no matter what you do, and there's no way to stop a speeding train, or in our case, a crawling car. That's the best way I can explain how I felt during those days on bedrest.

Did I have hope? Sure. I read success stories, people were praying for us, and we had great doctors. I had hope. But hope just couldn't outweigh the nagging feeling of dread, not to mention the facts and statistics. They were not on our side.

Also during this time, I read about a doctor in Florida who was attempting to seal women's torn and leaking amniotic sacs. My heart leapt out of my chest when I first saw the article. I could get to Florida! They could seal the tear shut. My babies were going to be OKAY! Of course, the treatment had about a one in a million chance of actually working. Oh, and it only worked for an amniotic sac that had a tiny tear and a slow leak, like one you might get from an amniocentesis. Mine was obviously busted right open, so it wasn't really an option. That didn't stop me from emailing them, telling them my story, and begging for help. I never did hear back, though.

Each day would bring a new twitch or pain and, along with it, the decision that this would be the day I went into labor. I begged Brian not to go to work. It was so difficult for him. He was full of fear, too, but he dealt with it by working and taking care of me. All day long I would analyze every single pain or cramp or feeling. Pregnancy, even a healthy one, comes with plenty of those, and so I spent a lot of my day wondering what was going on and reading anything and everything to help me try to figure them out.

I also spent many hours of those days reading articles online, researching PPROM, and putting baby clothes and items in my online shopping cart. I couldn't buy anything anymore, of course—that just seemed masochistic—but I wanted to. I had a stroller and a car seat and cribs already because I had gotten them at a great deal. We had even gone out and traded in our Jeep for a family van on the night of our twenty-week scan. Seeing those two healthy babies at twenty weeks made us so excited that as soon as the appointment was over, we immediately went to the car dealership and purchased the van we had been looking at. I have a great memory of leaving the dealership and driving straight to my mother-in-law's house. We pulled in the driveway and honked. We had done it! We had all the ultrasound pictures and a new van. You couldn't wipe the grins off of our faces.

It hurt so badly to look at everything now but not buy it. We had money saved and, of course, with my type A personality, I had lists of what I needed to buy. Brian had subscribed to *Consumer Reports*, so we knew we would have the top-rated baby gear. I spent my nights browsing articles online about babies and baby supplies and safety. We had the cribs put together and the room painted and two glider chairs all put together and ready. We purchased two because we figured we might each be feeding a baby in the night!

People from work signed up to bring us meals for as long as I was on bedrest. I don't think people had the real story about what happened; or if they did know, they were very good at seeming positive when they stopped by. I was very grateful for them, but I also dreaded the arrival of even the most well meaning of visitors because I didn't really want to see anyone. I felt so hopeless and alone, and I couldn't really describe what was happening.

Many people dropped by with magazines and books and offers of prayers. Our twins were on prayer lists from here to France. With so many people praying for them, I wondered, how could things go wrong?

There was one night when Brian made us dinner. He wasn't a very confident cook since I typically did all of the cooking, but he scoured the kitchen for ingredients that he was at least a little familiar with. That night he made us a meal fit for college kids—chicken nuggets and tater-tots. When he brought his masterpiece upstairs, I could see his eyes were filled with pride. He had put the ketchup and barbecue sauce in little tiny ramekins next to my grand meal, and cup of ice with a straw alongside my diet soda completed the picture. My favorite cookies were for dessert, and as he set the tray down next to me, he also set a napkin in my lap. I became completely overcome by emotion.

I couldn't hold it in anymore. My body couldn't handle the emotions, the sadness, and the fear. Brian thought he had done something wrong, of course. I couldn't get the words out, but this time the sadness wasn't about me or my pain; it was about him. Brian, my love, the man whom I had chosen to be the father of my children. I had chosen him for everything that I hadn't had in a father. He wanted more than anything to be a dad. The second I brought up being ready to try for a baby, he was on board. I had heard my friends' stories about husbands saying that it just wasn't time yet, or they couldn't afford it . . . not Brian. He was totally ready and just as excited as I was. He had the kindness, patience, and the level-headedness you need to be an amazing father.

I thought about how badly I wanted this for him. I wasn't much of a praying person at this point in my life, but I prayed right then. It was more like I begged. *God, I swear, look at this man. Please, please don't take these babies away from him. He would be the best dad you have ever known. He doesn't deserve this. Look at him. LOOK AT HIM. How could you possibly do this to him? He just lost his father and now this? PLEASE?* I kept saying the words in my mind as I cried. *Please, please, please. Just please don't take these babies away. We need them. He needs this.*

That night I needed to take a sleeping pill to settle myself down, and even then I still had nightmares the whole night. My recurring nightmare consisted of me wandering alone in a house until I heard a baby crying. I would continue walking until I would find a crib. Sometimes there would be two, three, or even four babies in the crib. But no matter how many babies there were, I couldn't touch them. Their cries tormented me. Their little bodies turned pink as they wailed. I stood next to the crib, devastated, because I couldn't reach them. There was no way for me to comfort them or settle them down. No matter what I did, I was stuck, waiting, unable to help.

To be sure, I was in a dark place. I spent a lot of my day crying. I couldn't get out of bed, and I really didn't want to see anyone. A few of my closest friends came, and with them they brought food, hope, and distraction. But it couldn't stop the darkness and the fear from creeping in as soon as they left.

And then there were the people who certainly did not help. Once, Brian woke me up to tell me that a coworker of his had stopped by with dinner and wanted to see me. She peeked around the corner as I tried to situate myself. But as I propped myself up, fluid gushed out and soaked my bed. I whimpered and then began to cry, asking for Brian. I was so distraught, I didn't even care who was standing there in my bedroom.

She looked at me, tilted her head, and said, "You really need to stop crying, you know. Being that upset could really hurt the babies."

I stared at her.

She didn't stop. "And you know, crying causes stress, and babies can feel that stress."

I wanted to reply with, "Oh, right, the fact that my water broke, that's not causing stress; it's just me crying. Me crying will be what kills my babies."

Instead, I just screamed for Brian. I whispered to him, "You need to make her leave. Please. Just make her go."

About a week after I was released, I got a call to go to the clinic to get the first of two steroid shots. These steroid shots are given during preterm labor to help babies' lungs develop more quickly. Officially twenty-three weeks pregnant, it was the earliest time these shots even had a chance of being effective. Dr. Sanders said from the beginning that until our babies were twenty-three weeks, they weren't considered "viable." They wouldn't even try to save them until they were at least that gestation. That meant that going into labor anytime before twenty-three weeks meant certain death.

As it turns out, different hospitals have different rules on this. Some hospitals don't consider a fetus viable until twenty-four weeks, some begin as early as twenty-two weeks. With each passing year, hospitals develop new technology that allows them to save babies born earlier and sicker.

Psychologically, reaching twenty-three weeks was the biggest milestone for me. I had it in my head that since we were still stable two weeks after my water broke, things really were going to be okay. Dr. Sanders showed us statistics that gave us even more hope; after twenty-four weeks, each week that went by made a HUGE difference in survival rates. At twenty-eight weeks, they would induce labor to lower my risk of infection and be able to save both babies. That was my plan. We were going all the way until week twenty-eight.

That day, after I had my steroid shot (which hurt like hell, yo!), we were also given a tour of the Neonatal Intensive Care Unit, otherwise known as the NICU. It was like all of a sudden everyone was treating us differently. We weren't just a hopeless, sad, pathetic case anymore. We had reached viability! We had hope! I was pushed around in a wheelchair, and we saw some parents sitting next to the incubators that held their sick or too small or injured infants. I pictured myself sitting next to an incubator and shook that vision right out of my head. They were staying in until it was time to come out.

We were also shown the delivery room we would use. It was directly across from the NICU so the babies would be able to be immediately transported there for care.

Returning home that day, I was, of course, exhausted and overwhelmed, but I felt a renewed strength. I wasn't as afraid anymore. I began making to-do lists again, and I even ordered a few things for the babies. At night when I couldn't sleep, I would lie in bed and talk to Sophie and Aiden.

"You guys. We've got this, okay? Mama is so proud of you. You're fighting so hard. I'm so gonna get you each a car when you're sixteen. It might not be a *great* car, but you will each have one. I promise!"

***

Easter Sunday was a big day for us. Still pregnant fourteen days after my water broke, I had gotten my steroid shots, and I even felt like I was leaking less fluid. I had a routine, and my mom and stepdad were coming for a visit, so I made sure to take a quick shower and get "dressed" for the day.

When my mom arrived, however, she immediately told me I didn't look good. My cheeks were red, she said. Sure, I agreed, I didn't feel the greatest, but I spent all of my time in a bed. How great *could* I feel? She looked me over again and told me that she didn't like my color and that my cheeks were really, *really* red.

Was I feeling ill? My cheeks were definitely hot pink, Brian agreed. I wrote furiously in my journal, making sure to note that I thought I felt fine. A colleague stopped by to bring us dinner, and I decided I would write all of my classes a note! You know, "Dear everyone, I miss you. I hope you're learning a lot!" That would help keep me busy and distracted. At the time, I taught six classes of first year French made up of sixth, seventh, and eighth graders. They were all so excited that I was pregnant with twins. I brought in all of the pictures from my ultrasound, and we brainstormed names at the end of class.

The distraction worked for a while, but I fell into a restless sleep that night. As the days went by, sleep was harder to come by because of how much time I spent in bed. I could already feel my muscles weakening from getting absolutely no exercise, and my hips ached all the way down to my bones.

Sometime around 4:30 or 5:00 a.m., I woke up with an unfamiliar discomfort. I hobbled into the bathroom and had a bowel movement. It hurt, and I felt funny. My mind flashed to the pregnancy binder page titled, "Warning Signs of Premature Delivery." I grabbed it off of the table next to me and flipped open to that section, which read:

It is extremely rare that a woman will go into premature labor. Most often, they are the same symptoms as indigestion or simple discomforts that go along with pregnancy. That said, here are some things to look for:

Flu-like symptoms (nausea/diarrhea/vomiting) (check)
Back pain (check)
Fluid leaking from your vagina (well . . . check)
Cramping (check)
Increased pressure (check)

The problem was that I had all of these symptoms all along. I truly didn't know what to think. I wanted to blame the Easter dinner that someone had brought that afternoon for causing my sour stomach, but I still had a nagging feeling.

After two more bowel movements and what I thought might be a contraction (how was I supposed to know?!), I woke Brian. We decided, together, to call labor and delivery. I didn't want to call. I was supposed to be deliriously happy when I called labor and delivery. I was supposed to call Brian and yell into the phone, "It's happening!!!" and have him race off to the hospital with a suitcase packed with our toothbrushes and two baby blankets. I was supposed to have a playlist on my iPod with motivational music, and there should have been two car seats installed. I think as much as I had been terrified and had experienced so much pain in the two weeks since my water broke, I had never let myself feel like any of it was real. But in that moment, dialing the number for labor and delivery felt like giving up. I was being forced to admit that this was, in fact, real—it was happening, and it was not going to be good. Still, the perinatologist had told me that I needed to get to twenty-three weeks gestation for the babies to be considered viable, and here I was at twenty-three weeks and three days. I had done it! We all had a fighting chance, right?

My initial call to labor and delivery was met with confusion. The first nurse I talked to said she wanted to get her supervisor. The next nurse, after putting me on hold several times, told me that I probably just had indigestion, and I should wait until 8:30 and call my doctor's office to be seen.

As soon as I hung up the phone, I had another cramp, and this time I was positive that it was a contraction. I started sobbing and told Brian we needed to go, even if they didn't think so. By the time we had our bags packed, someone from the hospital called back, out of breath, saying that they had called the on-call physician, and he said that we needed to go there immediately.

Nearing the hospital, a wave of panic came over me. I couldn't breathe. The entrance to the maternity ward is through the emergency room, and so I was hurriedly put in a wheelchair and rolled into the elevator. I felt like I was trapped in my own body, and I couldn't move. I was frozen, and as I was wheeled closer to a delivery room, I thought my lungs would burst before I could breathe again.

The first thing they did was draw my blood to check for infection. My doctor had mentioned earlier that, in the past, he had been able to deliver the twin whose water had broken but then try to stop labor to keep the second twin in utero. This gave the second twin's lungs more time to develop, but this would be dependent on *my* body being healthy.

I was given an IV and put in a hospital gown to wait while they monitored things. Watching the babies' heartbeats was always terrifying for me. In the two weeks that I was on bedrest, I had read countless stories about stillbirths and about there not being a heartbeat. I was sure that's what was coming next. Every time one of the babies' heartbeats would disappear or be difficult to find, my heart would thump so loudly I was sure everyone could hear it.

Within an hour, Dr. Sanders was back with news. He told me that my white blood cell count showed a terrible infection, and that meant there was no chance of trying to keep Baby B in after Baby A was born. I started crying, which I don't think he had the patience for. He looked me in the eye and said, "You need to deliver these babies. I can't tell you what's going to happen to them, but it is very early. Babies have about a ten to thirty-five percent survival rate when born at twenty-three weeks. But they have got to be delivered first. Now, we need to talk about how we can get them here."

"I want a C-section," I demanded. That had been decided days ago. I wanted a C-section. I did not want to push those tiny, fragile babies out of me. I was too weak. I couldn't do it. I didn't want to feel. I wanted drugs, and surgery, and not to feel.

"That's *really* not a good idea, Christine. You need to think about your future pregnancies. And unfortunately, in order to take care of your body for the future, you need to deliver these babies vaginally. You have to."

"SCREW YOU!" I screamed back. "You're not the one that has to DO IT!"

"I'll give you some time to discuss this with your husband," he replied, and left the room.

I reached over and pounded my fist on the hospital table, knocking a cup of ice chips off and causing it to rock dangerously back and forth, threatening to tip. "This is FUCKING BULLSHIT!" I raged. "I CANNOT DO THIS!"

It was the labor and delivery nurse who eventually convinced me that I could, and I would. She sat down next to me and held my hand. She rubbed my palm with her fingers as she explained what the doctor had meant about future pregnancies. "Honey, this isn't a good idea because you are going to want to have other babies someday. And bodies don't like to deliver babies after they've already had Cesarean sections. I know you can't think past today, past this minute, but this is just what you have to do today. Mothers, they do impossible things, and that's what you'll do."

They pushed me to the delivery room closest to the NICU, and the NICU team came in to meet me and ask me some questions. Everything was instantly chaotic as they moved bed parts to transition my bed from a hospital bed to a delivery bed. I tried to follow instructions as the team shot questions at me.

"Do you want your children to receive heroic life-saving measures?"

"Would you like to know the survival rate statistics at this point?"

"How important is it to you to hold the baby while he or she is still alive?"

"We. We . . . guess so. Yes. We think so. Yes, we do want heroic measures," I tripped over my words. They sounded insane coming out of my mouth. Heroic measures? What the hell does that even *mean?* I almost laughed, picturing Superman swooping in to save my babies.

They told us they would do *everything they could.* I didn't really understand what I was saying 'yes' to. I mean, I understood the questions. I could comprehend the words being said to me. But, there's no way to *really* know what they are talking about. Who could ever be prepared for this? I really thought that since I had stayed pregnant, it wouldn't be this way. I had passed twenty-three weeks, which I thought meant things would be better. Those of you reading this who have had a preemie or know what a twenty-three-week-old baby looks like, you'd know that *of course* things were dire. *Of course* you would know that having a baby that tiny would involve something devastatingly heroic.

Everything they could. Well, what couldn't doctors do? You could give someone a face transplant, or a new leg, or something to pump his heart. But, as it turns out, there's just still a lot we can't do. There were some things that were ONLY up to me, my body, and I had failed at them all. The job of growing those babies had been mine.

My nurse was an absolute and complete angel. I cannot remember her name, and I have only a very fuzzy recollection of what she looked like. But I remember her calming voice and her soft hands. I remember her skin smelled a little like baby powder. Mostly, I remember screaming over and over, "I can't do this. Please don't make me. I can't." And every time, without fail, she would grab my hand and look me right in the eyes and state, "Yes. You can. And you will."

She never left my side. Brian paced next to my bed, looking so scared and alone. He was lost, and, truthfully, not really sure what was happening. But this woman, this nurse, she saved my life that day. Over and over, she stood and took my anger and fear, and she held steady and reminded me that I could do this.

My doctor was one of the best in terms of knowledge, and he's who I wanted making decisions for me, but he lacked a lot in bedside manner. While I am sure that in his line of work he had to desensitize himself to the fact that little, tiny babies die every day, his brain was all about the numbers and the data: "Mr. and Mrs. Wopat, eleven percent of twins are born weighing less than three pounds in this country, you know." So he would come in and out while I was laboring, grab my foot out of a stirrup, and announce how many centimeters I was dilated.

Toward the end, the doctor came in and pulled an ultrasound machine next to me. "Looks like we're ready to push here. You're a full ten. Here we go."

I started to bear down and push.

"Wait! Christine, you have to wait until the next contraction comes before you push. Can you feel the contractions with the epidural?"

I nodded.

You only push when there are contractions? My mind wandered to the labor and delivery class I had registered for and never taken. I thought of how pregnant women on TV always went to Lamaze class and sat on the floor, practicing their breathing while their husband sat behind them with a pillow, looking frightened.

I pushed Sophie Mae Wopat out at 12:40 p.m., and I didn't even get to see her. The head NICU doctor immediately wrapped her in a blanket and whisked her away. I didn't even know that she weighed one pound and six ounces until I got her death certificate. The doctor reminded me to keep pushing so that Baby B could make his way down.

The doctor went back and forth between checking me and moving the ultrasound around. "You never can trust the second twin," he said.

A few minutes later, I was mid-push and someone came running in. "Do you want your daughter baptized?"

I looked at Brian, too confused to answer, too concerned with pushing to stop and register the question.

He was silent. "Babe?"

Rage built up inside of me. *I CANNOT DO ALL OF THIS*, I screamed, inside my head.

"NO!" I screamed. Literally, out loud, screamed.

"Mrs. Wopat. Your daughter, she . . . she's not doing well. I'm not sure we can do anything at this point. We've tried to resuscitate her several times . . . but . . . Mrs. Wopat, Christine, do you want your daughter baptized?"

I looked at Brian, rage in my eyes. "I'm doing all the work over here. You tell the lady her answer." My perinatologist was muttering things about the "second twin" and trying to ultrasound my belly to make sure he hadn't flipped around.

Brian told them 'no.' I have never asked him why, but my guess is that saying 'yes' felt like admitting defeat. I don't know what I would have said. If we gave permission for a baptism, we were saying it was okay for her to die. And I still hadn't even delivered my second baby.

She looked at us long and hard, and then she left. I have a feeling they baptized Sophie anyway. I mean, I probably would have. She had to know that we had no idea what we were doing.

The doctor continued his back-and-forth between me and the ultrasound machine. "You never can trust the second twin," he repeated, probably ten times. "The second one always likes to make things more interesting. Gotta keep watching."

Aiden James Wopat was born at 1:09 p.m., and he came out wiggling and moving all around, nice and pink. He was tiny—one pound and eight ounces—but absolutely full of life. They wrapped him in a blanket and held him up close to me so I could see him. The doctor grinned at me. "That's what we like to see! He's looking great! You've got a fighter." And then Aiden, too, was taken away to the NICU, leaving us all alone.

CHAPTER 3 - PAIN MANAGEMENT

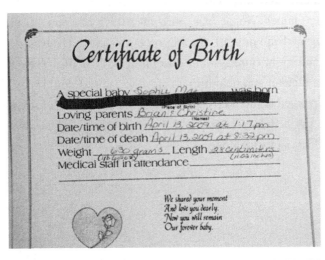

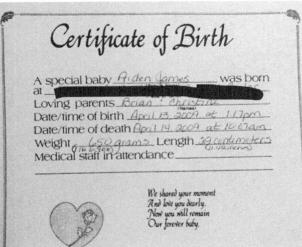

When the time finally came when we could visit the NICU, I suddenly freaked out. I didn't want to go. I know that sounds awful, like what mother wouldn't want to go and meet her own brand-new baby? But I was terrified, more scared than I had ever been in my life, and so confused about what was actually happening. On top of the mental and physical exhaustion that comes with labor and childbirth, there was a collective understanding that the situation was dire. There was a feeling of impending doom.

Brian wheeled me out of the room, and we headed down a long corridor. My legs began to shake uncontrollably even though I was sitting, and tears sprang instantly to my eyes. The warped wooden floors creaked under the weight of my wheelchair. The hallway had the subtle odor of disinfectant and stale air, and I had to look away from giant portraits of beautiful, cherub-like babies resting on their mothers' chests.

Once you get into the NICU, you have to use special soap to wash your hands and arms and put covers on your shoes. We signed in and followed all of the sanitation instructions, and then we just waited, awkwardly, for someone to tell us what to do. All around us were neonatal incubators, little closed-in beds made of plastic with holes so you could reach in. Seeing them felt like someone was stepping on my chest and refusing to let up. A nurse saw us and led us to Sophie's isolette first.

At first glance, she looked so unbelievably tiny and sick and very red. Babies this premature in gestation still definitely look like babies, just not the chubby, jolly kind you're used to seeing. Sophie looked tiny but cute. I could see my features in her—my funny shaped, extra-large nose and indented chin. Her eyes were still closed, and I wondered what color they would be. Hazel like mine or blue like her dad's?

I reached my hand into the circular hole on one side and brushed a finger to her sweet little hand. Shockingly, she took hold of my finger with her tiny hand and squeezed. In that moment, motherhood overtook me. I had created this baby, this person. And whether or not she would live didn't matter anymore. My love for her was mountainous. I could sense her quiet and shy demeanor. I knew that she was stubborn and would totally get her way with both me and her father.

I imagined what it would be like to brush long, thick, curly hair or to buy her a teddy bear. And with that, I couldn't hold it together anymore. In that one moment, in that one touch, my brain had ignited an inferno of need. Every fiber in my being was desperate to hold her. We should escape. Run like the wind, run away from this ridiculous hospital and all of the wires and alarms and sterilizing soap.

Next came fury. I was FURIOUS with myself for not protecting her and not taking care of her. I was insane with anger about the fact that she should still be inside the womb, growing and developing, but instead she was in this machine that had over twenty tubes and wires and electrodes sticking out all over. How could I have done this to her, and she still reached out and grabbed my finger? She was here, and she was alive, and she was a person. This actually became my mantra for the first few years after Sophie and Aiden died. They were here, they were alive, they were people.

The NICU doctor came over and stood beside me. "I didn't think we would get her stabilized," she admitted. "She held my finger like that, too. She's a sweet girl, that daughter of yours."

I stood there for a moment, letting those words wash over me. *She's a sweet girl.* That daughter of mine. *That daughter of mine.* My sweet Sophie, who had been kicking at my ribs for the last two weeks. Who was awake at night and liked to take naps all day. Sophie, who would kick like mad for some chocolate.

I can't say how long we waited there. I noticed a couple across the way, sitting next to their baby, and I made eye contact with them. This baby seemed to have been a patient for a while; there were stuffed animals and name tags and photos taped all around her little station. My eyes must have given away my fear because the woman smiled at me. "You'll get used to it," she said. "The alarms and all that. After a while, they fade away."

Of course at the time I thought, "I'll never get used to this." How do you sit next to your baby in an incubator, not being able to hold her, not knowing if she will live or die. But what I wouldn't give now to have had that chance. There is so much I would give for that chance, even for just a day to sit next to her, to cradle her, to get to know her.

I had only been next to her for a few minutes when alarms started sounding. The cacophony of sound overtook me. Lights were blinking, and everyone in the entire NICU immediately abandoned what they were doing and rushed over. It took me several moments to realize that the alarms were sounding from Sophie's machines.

I had a panic attack right there in my wheelchair. I couldn't breathe. My heart seemed to stop working. I managed to whisper, hoarsely, to my husband, "Get me out of here. Take me back to the room." Brian just stood there, so I got up out of my chair and started walking toward the hallway. He managed to rush after me and sit me back down in the chair. I urged him to hurry, and we raced back to our hospital room, where I sat, heaving and sobbing, barely able to take in breaths.

Within minutes, a NICU nurse was at my door. "Ma'am, excuse me, but you need to come back now. You need to come in. We are losing your daughter."

Brian started to pull my wheelchair back, and I screamed, "NO! I am NOT going back in there! If we go back in there, then this is over. It's done."

We had a silent standoff—the NICU nurse, my husband, and me. I looked at them both, daring them. There was a curt nod, and the nurse turned and walked out. Brian slowly wheeled me toward the door. My shoulders fell. I had no more fight in me.

My mind was oddly empty of thoughts as we made our way back to watch our baby die. My knee bounced, and I can remember watching beads of sweat pooling on Brian's brow.

As we rounded the corner, I noticed that the entire NICU was eerily silent and almost empty. The last few terrified-looking parents were filing into a small room in the back corner. The NICU nurses were all lined up, almost like a firing squad, against one wall. Medical carts and trays made a barrier around Sophie's incubator, making the whole room seem smaller and darker. *This is what death looks like,* I thought.

It felt like the entire world was screeching to a halt as we re-washed our hands and put on new booties over our shoes.

As we finished, a nurse came up and put her hand on my shoulder. She said gently, quietly, "We're going to take your daughter out of her isolette now and remove all of the wires so you can hold her."

She led me to a rocking chair that was waiting in the middle of the room. I sat down, reluctantly, and not at all gracefully. "Her little lungs just couldn't do it," the doctor explained as she began to open the isolette. "But she sure fought hard."

It took a thousand years for her to get Sophie all the way out and free of her wires. I cringed every time something got tangled around her tiny little body, and I found it sickeningly humorous that I worried about her getting hurt by wires since she was already in the middle of dying.

Wrapped in a blanket, she was set tenderly in my arms. I noticed that she had adorable ears and that she had a bracelet around her leg that said, "Baby Girl Wopat, Baby A." I held her, awkwardly and stupidly, totally clueless.

Sophie and Aiden were my first babies. I didn't know anything about what it was like to have one to hold, or what you were supposed to do with them. I didn't know how to find the right crook in your arm for the baby's head to rest. If I knew then what I know now, I would have kissed her all over. I would have asked to give her a bath and change her into her baptismal gown, and I would have held her in my lap and really looked at her. I would have done a million things differently. I held her like she was a china doll, like she would just break in half. I held her stiffly while the doctor reached over every few minutes to take her pulse, which was slowing down each time. I held her, but I didn't really *hold* her. Not like a mom should hold her newborn daughter. That was all taken from me, robbed from me without warning or cause.

My husband stood behind me and cried. He couldn't hold her. He was too afraid, and honestly, I don't blame him. He is the best dad, and a loving husband, and he would do anything for his children or me, but he couldn't bring himself to hold her. To understand pain is to understand that decision.

At some point, the doctor looked at his watch, with his fingertips on Sophie, and in a slow, steady voice, he stated, "Time of death, 20:32."

I looked at a nurse and pleaded, "Please take her. Please take her." And I handed her over. And I never saw her again. Never again. I have replayed those moments in my mind thousands of times. Why did I give her back so quickly? Why didn't I take in those moments and keep them for myself instead of giving her back?

No one said anything to me, so I ditched my wheelchair and shuffled as best I could to my hospital room, with Brian following close behind. My mom sat up when I entered the room. I managed to utter, "Sophie is dead," and then I curled up on my bed and stared at the wall. "At least we still have Aiden," I said, to no one in particular.

It was hours before anyone came back in to talk to us. My mom coaxed me into a bath, and a nurse came in and out to check my vitals and make sure my recovery was going okay and to help me manage pain. Pain management. Hilarious.

Brian left at one point to be with his mom out in the waiting room, and when he came back he was clutching a folder in his hand. "What's that?" I asked, and he placed the folder on the bed next to me. Inside the folder was a glossy, colorful brochure for a non-profit organization, *Now I Lay Me Down to Sleep*. Volunteer photographers would come to take tasteful, beautiful photographs of your family with your baby—

even if your baby had died.

At that exact moment, a hospital employee walked in the room. "Oh, good, you got the folder, " he said. "Should I set up an appointment for you with a photographer? They do great work."

"No!" I blurted, then I tried to be more polite. "No, thank you." Pictures felt...strange. Now, of course, I could kick myself for passing up an amazing opportunity like that.

The hospital worker continued, "Okay. Let me know if you change your mind. There should also be a postcard inside the folder. Please put that on your door. I'll be back to check on you guys soon."

The postcard was a photograph of a red and brown leaf and a dew drop making ripples in the water. There were no other words on it, just the leaves and dew drops. I turned it over and realized what it was. It all started to sink in. It was essentially a "My Baby Died" sign for my door. Brian shrugged at me. "I guess we should put it up?" I turned back toward the wall.

Close to midnight, a NICU physician stopped in. "Hi, folks. I'm very sorry, but I wanted to let you know that you won't be allowed to visit the NICU overnight. We are closing it off to all parents, barring an emergency. This is because your son, Aiden, needs a lot of help. We'll try to keep you updated, but please call for updates if you feel it's been too long. Do you have any questions?"

We could only stare. After the physician left, my mom curled up on a chair in the corner, and Brian had a hospital bed next to mine. They were drifting in and out of sleep, but my body wouldn't even consider it.

I busied myself trying to use a breast pump several times, but next to nothing came out. The nurse stayed positive, cheerfully putting one drop of colostrum into a vial and announcing, "This is liquid gold!" each time I finished.

Throughout the night we had visitors updating us about Aiden. We had to sign paperwork for him to get blood transfusions and other procedures. Nothing looked good. There was no good news.

But, with morning light came hope. It had been a few hours since we had seen or heard from anyone. I picked up the phone and dialed the number to the NICU.

"Hello, NICU," came a voice through the phone.

"Uh, hello," I said. "I'm um, I'm calling about Aiden . . . uh, Wopat?"

"Sure thing, may I ask who is calling?"

"This is . . . uh, well, this is . . . his, his . . . mom." The words didn't feel right as they stumbled out. I felt like an imposter, someone posing as a mother.

"Oh, okay. Well, Aiden made it through the night. You and your husband should feel free to come on down and have a visit as soon as you are able."

I don't remember much of my visit with Aiden that morning. I do remember that he looked good to me, better than his sister. His coloring was different, less red. I was able to hold his hand and sing to him. However, they had him attached to a machine that made it difficult to be near him. His lungs were severely underdeveloped, and the machine vibrated rapidly to help his lungs take small breaths. His whole body shook.

We couldn't stay long, they said, because Aiden needed tests and another blood transfusion. We went back to the room to rest and eat. Medication and not eating for so long had made me nauseous, and I was still very sore and bleeding heavily. I continued to try the breast pump, but to no avail. Just another part of me that was broken, I decided.

I slept fitfully, begrudgingly, for a few hours. Everything I did felt wrong.

***

Later that afternoon, we had just walked back into the NICU when we saw that our family doctor, Dr. Brown, was scrubbing in as well.

"He's looking good, you guys," she said, as she came over to us. She wrapped me in a hug and whispered to me, "I'm so sorry. I'm so, so sorry." Her presence gave me momentary peace.

A few minutes later, my mom joined us to visit the baby. We all took turns looking at him, talking to him, and holding his hand. As we stood there, Brian and I discussed how we would handle Aiden's long NICU stay. "You'll just take your maternity leave," Brian said. "And as soon as work is done, I'll come down for a visit, too. We can take turns staying the night when they'll let us." I didn't know when I'd be discharged from the hospital, but the staff had already told us that when things were slow in the maternity wing, sometimes NICU parents could sleep in the rooms.

We were getting ready to go back to the room so I could lie down when one of Aiden's alarms went off. I flinched a little, but I wasn't really even worried. He looked good! He came out squirming! He was a fighter!

Dr. Brown stepped out of the way as more alarms started sounding. I looked around, watching the other parents look at us with pity in their eyes. A young man came up to me and said, "He is failing. Our attempts to resuscitate him are not working. Do you want us to try CPR again?"

I thought, "How in the world can you even *do* CPR on a baby so tiny?" These decisions, one after the other, were destroying me. I was so wrecked that I couldn't form words. I rubbed my eyes.

The man looked at me. "Ma'am, I'm sorry, but what would you like us to do? We can try again, but you need to tell us."

At that moment, something just came over me. In one wave, my fear left me, and anger swept over me. Sadness and grief, and I think for the first time, I just owned the fact that I was, in fact, someone's mother. I was someone's mother, and they needed me to make the right decision.

"No," I said. "No, please don't do that. Please stop the alarms and let me hold my son." My voice shook as I said it, but in that moment, I knew it's what was right for my baby. I knew that even if CPR worked, which seemed doubtful, he would need it again, or something else would go wrong. I had read countless stories over the last few weeks about babies who had survived after being born at twenty-three weeks, but mine wouldn't be one of them. We wouldn't get to be a survivor story. Of course there are days when I regret that decision. I have hated myself and let guilt completely own me for making that call. I think there will always be something nagging in the back of my mind, a "what if" that will always haunt me. But most days, I do believe that I did the right thing. Most days I know that it wouldn't have mattered— that he was going to die no matter what. I did find out later on that his placenta was also infected, which was why some of the treatments weren't working. I guess that helps a little, too. But honestly, I know deep down that no matter what I decided that day, it was the right decision because I was acting as Aiden's mom. I remember that at some point in the night that Aiden was in the NICU, a nurse came into my room and asked, "You're Aiden's mom, right?" and I felt this tremendous surge of joy come over me. Me, having just lost my daughter and unable to breastfeed and bleeding, was able to feel a moment of joy. I had fought so hard to become somebody's mother. And even if it was only for a few hours, and even under those terrible circumstances, it felt miraculous.

I wish I could tell you that I did things differently with Aiden. That after having a half-day to think about it, I had figured out what I should do with my dying baby, but I didn't. Someone brought him a tiny baptismal gown and carefully placed him in it. We couldn't find the chaplain, so my mom got a little decorative shell from the table, filled it with water, and walked over to Aiden in his isolette. She dipped her finger lightly in the shell, and a dabbed a little drop of water on his tiny forehead. "Dear Aiden," she sobbed, "I baptize you in the name of the Father, the Son, and the Holy Ghost." Our heads hung down, the pain gathering up inside of me like a storm, ready to unleash its fury.

It was like some sort of strange alternate universe when the nurses put the barricades back up and asked all of the other parents to leave. I know it must have been terrifying for them, seeing this happen to the same people, twice, in such a short time. I admit that I have blocked a lot of this scene out of my memory. What I remember the most is that Dr. Brown, who had just stopped by to see me, stood in that room the entire time. When the time came for me to sit down and rock my dying baby, that woman stood right behind me with her hand on my shoulder. And as I sobbed and rocked and screamed, "I'm so sorry. I'm so sorry, baby. Mommy is so sorry that she couldn't keep you safe," she kept her hand there, and she firmly repeated, "Christy, this is not your fault. This is NOT your fault." I will, forever and always, be in awe of her and be grateful for her. Throughout this entire experience, I had all different kinds of doctors, but the kindness and strength that she showed me during those moments was never rivaled.

"Time of death: 10:07."

I let loose a sound from the very core of me that shook the room. I let loose from my very core, my primal self, the sound of total and complete emptiness, the sound of utter despair and loss, the sound of a future ripped from my hands as swiftly as it was given to me, and never, ever can I forget that sound. Shattered, my heart fragmented into a thousand tiny pieces at that moment, and the scream of broken glass slamming the cold, hard floor echoed through my soul, and I knew, in that instant, that even if I could put the pieces back together again, there would always be dusty little fragments, and they would always be missing. We would never be whole. Ever.

I handed Aiden back to the nurse and glanced over at my husband, my best friend, who looked so scared and shocked. I didn't even know what to say. I didn't know what to do. I didn't want to know what would happen next. Would Aiden go to a morgue? Is that where Sophie was?

We slowly left the NICU after that, just wanting to escape, I guess. The perinatologist was out in the hallway. "You guys, I am so surprised to hear about this unfortunate turn of events. I really thought he was a fighter." I just kept walking. I didn't have time for him, and honestly, I was getting pissed about the fact that people said he was *not* a fighter. Just because he died didn't mean he didn't fight. And, he shouldn't have *had* to fight. That was on me.

The doctor, however, followed us to the room. He sat down in a chair and pulled it up to the edge of the bed. "We're sending some things over to the lab to try to get some more answers. I want to see you in my office in two weeks. In the meantime, is there anything I can do for you now?"

I knew exactly what I wanted—to get as far away from that hospital as I could. "I want to get discharged from this hospital as fast as I can. I want to leave." He nodded and said he would see to it.

About an hour and a half later, a nurse came in with the discharge papers. This is a moment that has stayed with me all of these years. She sat down right next to me, and she held my hand. And then she took out a folder (with the lovely dew drop dead baby leaf on it), and from it she pulled out a brochure. And she read a list of discharge instructions for "couples who have experienced pregnancy loss." As she read the list, tears streamed down her face. She would squeeze my hand or my knee and look directly into my eyes. I like people who can look a grieving mother right in the eyes.

"You may experience pain from your milk ducts clogging. Use ice packs to help with that. You may not have intercourse for at least six weeks. And you may not be ready, emotionally, even then. Be there for each other. Hug each other. Talk. Take walks, holding hands . . ."

We listened, and we nodded. And then we took the folder, grabbed our suitcase, and we walked out of that hospital, not pregnant, without any babies.

CHAPTER 4 - DEAD BABY MOM

From: Funeralhome@email.com
Subject: Re: Inquiry
Date: April 15, 2009
To: christywopat@email.com

Hello Christy,

We received your inquiry about the cremation services we offer. I wanted to let you know that we do offer cremation services for infants. However, since their bodies are so tiny, we have to cremate them at the same time as an adult. If we tried to do it alone, their bodies would burn too quickly. We can get this process started for you, but I cannot promise the ashes quickly, as we need to wait for someone else who needs cremation.

At your convenience, we'd like you to come down to choose urns for your babies. We have several different options at different cost levels.

As for your inquiry about cost, we do not charge for infant cremation, we only charge for the urns. Please feel free to call us whenever you are available, and we'll look for you to come down to make some decisions.

Would you also be interested in a memorial service at all? We have many families choose to do this, and we can do it at any cost.

Thank you,
J. Richards

From: christywopat@email.com
Subject: Re:Re: Inquiry
Date: April 15, 2009
To: Funeralhome@email.com

Mr. Richards,

Thank you for your help. We will be down soon to pick out urns for the babies' ashes. We are not interested in a memorial at this time—I don't think I could survive it.

Have a nice day,
Christy Wopat

I was actually relieved to be going away from the hospital, away from the crying babies and the happy parents. As we left the hospital, I tried to avert my eyes from the moms being pushed in wheelchairs who were balancing flowers and pink and blue gift bags and balloons while their husbands gingerly carried infant car seats with sleeping babies tucked inside.

The ride home took years. It's hard to describe, this feeling of being pushed and pulled through some sort of a time warp, honestly not knowing what could ease the horrible pain that grips you. Once we arrived at our house, Brian put the car in park and looked at me. He put his hand on mine and tried to look me in the eyes. I couldn't. I had failed him, had failed at the one job in this world that only women are created to accomplish. I was a failure.

When I crossed the threshold, I was instantly sucker punched. Death confronted me from every corner of my house. On the kitchen counter was a pink and blue gift bag with a pair of baby booties I had been given on the day before I went into labor. The stack of mail contained coupons from Gerber along with a bill from the hospital for my initial stay. The mail was a constant barrage of reminders for many months after that—everything from baby coupons to sympathy cards to brand new health insurance cards that had "Aiden James" listed as our third family member. Evidently, Sophie hadn't been alive long enough to be added to our insurance policy. Formula samples, letters addressed to Aiden and Sophie, and then began the serious hospital bills, the ones for the delivery and NICU stay. Always hospital bills. Two babies in the NICU for only twenty-four hours costs a lot more than you might imagine.

Upstairs was worse. My heart sank as I reached my bedroom, still haunted by bedrest. I stood in the frame of the doorway, and my right leg shook as I took it all in. The mini fridge and the table pulled up next to my bed. Pitchers of water, magazines, and books stacked all over the folding table. *What to Expect When You're Expecting* glared at me from the bottom of the stack. The bedroom and bathroom light had been left on, and there were clothes strewn all over. Our bed was messy, and the whole room smelled damp like a basement. It was spring in Wisconsin, which meant melting snow everywhere and a need to air out the house of the stale winter air.

The door to the nursery had been pulled shut. Spontaneously, I walked up to it and shoved it open. I don't know what possessed me, but it was a really fucking terrible idea. As soon as I opened it, I felt as though someone had kicked me right in the chest. I sat down on the floor and let the grief roll over me like a wave. My whole body ached with the pain of losing my babies, and I couldn't keep any of it in. Not anymore.

My husband ran a hot bath and helped me in. As the steam rose up from the tub, I pulled my knees up to my chest and rocked back and forth, my screams echoing in the small room. "Give me my BABIES BACK!" I wailed over and over. "Why did this happen to ME?" I couldn't stop. Sobs wracked my body, and I couldn't slow down the words that flowed painfully from my soul. I slammed my fists against the walls of the bathtub and kicked the water, splashing it everywhere. I screamed until my voice was hoarse. The primal, down-to-your-core agony that had overtaken me was almost unbearable. Until that very moment, I had no idea how physically painful grief could feel. I had known deep sadness in my life: an estrangement with my father; a wicked, drawn-out divorce between my parents; the loss of three of my grandparents; and most recently my struggle with infertility concurrent with the loss of Brian's father after a nasty battle with cancer. None of it compared to this.

Brian stayed with me, by the side of the bathtub, and rubbed my back or held my hand or wiped water from my eyes. "I love you," he whispered, over and over. He would softly answer me with, "I don't know. I don't know why you. Why us." As much as I loved him in that moment, I could barely handle his touch. It reminded me of the life that was no longer inside of me. I remember often looking down in those early days and weeks to see how floppy and soft my belly had become. While I had never been a thin person, during pregnancy I felt *so* beautiful—glamorous, almost. I loved feeling my hard, round belly. I loved, for those fleeting months, seeing myself in the mirror or seeing a candid photograph of myself. Now, I hated every part of my empty self more than ever.

When I was shaking from the cold, and the skin on my fingertips was wrinkled from being in the water for so long, Brian eased me out of the tub to help me dress and get into bed. Once he seemed satisfied that I was calm, he began to busy himself in an attempt to put our bedroom back to its pre-trauma state. He took down the table and tossed out the magazines. I watched him gather up stacks of baby books and disappear for a moment. He would return and grab something else, then off he would go again.

Things popped up after that, certainly—the memories could never truly be put away, not even the tangible ones. I'd open a book, and a to-do list would fall out. "Love the sleigh crib from Amazon, check on price!/Call Julia and ask her about tandem nursing/Do we have fluoride in our water?" They would be crumpled and tossed in the garbage with vengeance. *Who gives a shit about fluoride in our water, anyway?*

Later I found out that he took all of those baby things and shoved them in a closet in the twins' nursery. According to him, it seemed like the only place that he could be sure I wouldn't see them until I was ready, and he thought I might be angry if he were to permanently get rid of any of them. He was right, of course, and there is not a day that goes by that I don't thank my lucky stars that he was my partner in all of this. Not a day.

I took some generic, over-the-counter sleeping pills that night but still wasn't able to sleep. A nice doctor somewhere had written me a prescription for an anxiety medication in case I was struggling, but I vowed not to fill it if I didn't have to. Looking back, I sometimes wish I would've taken it. I don't know what I was trying to prove. My anxiety was all-consuming and sleep was so difficult to achieve in those early days. On the other hand, feeling the pain made what happened feel real, and I could hang onto that.

That night I felt a phantom kick for the first time. Phantom kicks afflicted me for many weeks thereafter. I had grown so used to feeling Sophie and Aiden kick that the sensation was my companion at night. When I was pregnant, I would lay in bed watching television and rub my belly. Sometimes my babies would react to my hand pressing in a certain spot. But the ghostly kicks started the night we came home from the hospital, and they quite honestly made me feel crazy. My first, irrational, reckless thought was, "They were wrong. The babies are still in there! They're okay!" I was scared to mention them to my doctor because I thought she would have me committed to a mental institution. It wasn't until weeks later, when I connected with other bereaved mothers online, that I found out it's totally common. In fact, I had them to a lesser extent after my two subsequent "normal" pregnancies. You know, the kind where you get to bring the baby home.

The next morning I woke up with *that* feeling. You know the one— the one where after something bad happens, you wake up, and you've kind of forgotten, but something nags at you. And then it hits you all over again, and you just want it to have been a bad dream, but it's not. Yep. That one. Brian was already awake, and he was outside tinkering in the garage. I grabbed my computer and went online. An idea was forming in my mind. We live about an hour and a half drive from a tourist town called the Wisconsin Dells. It's full of hotels, water parks, and cheesy tourist activities, and it's one of my favorite places.

"Babe," I said. "You wanna go to the Dells? I found a deal online, and we could just go and get completely and totally away from here."

He looked at me and let a laugh escape, but caught himself when he realized I wasn't smiling. I took a big breath and kept going. "I really hate being here right now, and I'm afraid that people are going to come here, and everything here makes me want to crawl into a hole. I have no clothes that fit me, we have no food, and within a day, the funeral home is going to be calling here for decisions that I don't want to make. Can't make. Please, let's escape. Just for a little while."

And so we did. I used to think that running away wouldn't solve your problems, but I'm telling you that sometimes it (temporarily) can. The memory of those days is hazy but (dare I say?) pleasant. I was definitely hurting—both physically and mentally—but I don't think that things had completely settled into either of our heads yet. We were in shock.

We went shopping, we gorged on candy and junk food, and lay in bed watching trashy reality TV. We went to the movies and out to dinner, and even without an appetite, I ate. I cried through most of it. In the dark movie theater, in the aisles at the grocery store, I cried. Everywhere we went, I held Brian's hand and let him protect me. Thankfully, I didn't see a single soul I knew, and I avoided any kind of eye contact with strangers so that I didn't have to field a single question.

Nights at the hotel were the worst. Lying in bed felt so foreign to me. There was no belly to rub, no kicks to feel, no aching hips to complain about. A touch from my husband could cause a myriad of reactions: anxiety, pain, heartache, fear. Having him close to me was imperative—but not *too* close, you see.

When it was finally time to check out and go home, I felt more ready. I had regained just a little strength, but enough that I could face at least the beginning of this horrific journey. Many people judged us for leaving right away, including people in my immediate family. I guess I can understand. It must have looked strange that we were going on "vacation" in the face of a tragedy, but I challenge people to look past that and see that we were trying to cope in any way we could. It's not like there is a handbook for this, or a set of rules somewhere about what to do when your baby dies. I had no idea what to do, but what I *did* know was that I needed to be away. It was just the first in a long list of times when our family and friends passed judgment on what we were doing and how we were doing it. I have gained an incredible amount of strength and confidence because of this, for which I am grateful. I have learned that while you absolutely need to take other people's feelings into consideration in life, there are times when you have to really and truly only take care of yourself. Do what is going to be good and healing for you, and do it without worrying about what others will think.

The next few days were a blur—I didn't want to see anyone, and so I mostly just burrowed as far into a cocoon of blankets on my bed as I could. Brian went back to work right away, but my doctor felt that I shouldn't, and I was not about to argue with that. At the time, I taught middle school, and there were *seven* other teachers on staff who were pregnant at the same time as I was. I had also shared a lot with my students, and they had been excited along with me. I brought my ultrasound pictures in after my twenty week checkup, and we had a big poster where kids could write what they thought the twins' names should be. Everyone in that school knew that I was pregnant with twins, and if I had a medical excuse not to go back and face that, I took it. It was unpaid leave, but my husband was supportive, and really, in the thickness of grief, money is practically inconsequential.

Not to mention the obvious, but I had just given birth to two babies. Many people didn't (and still don't) understand that I labored. Contracted. Dilated to ten centimeters. Got an epidural. Pushed out babies and placentas. I bled everywhere and started leaking colostrum. Physically, I was nowhere near ready to return to work.

About a week after delivery, I stepped in the shower, and as the water heated up, I began to feel dizzy. I held onto the walls as the room began to spin, and when I looked down, I saw red. Passing under my feet toward the drain was a blood clot about the size of a lemon. The bleeding started coming steadily and heavily, and I managed to stumble out of the bathroom and wrap a towel around my waist.

The bleeding wouldn't stop, and I was also just scared about everything, so into the emergency room I went. I remember calling the high school where my husband worked, sobbing, begging Brian to meet me at the hospital. I was exhausted and weak and gushing blood, and still I would have preferred having a root canal without anesthesia to entering that hospital again.

This was my first real experience with post-loss doctor visits and the absolute shit that came along with them. As I entered triage, a nurse asked me to explain my symptoms. He looked at my chart.

"Well, I see you just delivered twins. Are you breastfeeding or bottle feeding?" He didn't look up from his computer.

There were so many times like this that I would imagine making up my own business cards. I could hand one to the doctor/mailman/hair stylist/dentist and wait for them to read it. I thought about including a ton of superfluous information like address, phone, website, a cute picture, whatever. Or maybe just something like this:

Christy Wopat
Dead Baby Mom

That's how we talked about ourselves sometimes. Me and the other moms I met online, later on, through our blogs. I'd say, "Oh, that's Angela, she's another Dead Baby Mom." I can see that it may sound morbid to phrase it like that. Sometimes I think we were trying to own that word *dead*—to make it ours so that we could be a little shocking. I was always (and still am) a little off-put by the use of the phrase, "She lost the baby."

When we talk about death, we use all sorts of euphemisms in an attempt to soften the blow in an effort to try to make everyone around us feel better. When we say, "I lost twins at twenty-four weeks," it just doesn't have the same impact as, "I had twins. They lived in the hospital for a few days. And then they died."

Lost. I lost my keys. I lost my passport. I lost my twins. They're not around somewhere, and I can't find them. They're gone. They're . . . dead. I know. Once, when I Googled something like, "My baby is dead," I found a whole website devoted to dead baby jokes. Jokes, intended to make people laugh, about dead babies. What in the *hell* is wrong with people?

I guess when we say we are dead baby moms, or baby loss moms, we are just trying to own who we are. To take it for ourselves. I wanted to hand out those business cards that just said, "Yo—my babies died. Stop asking me stupid questions and making me explain myself." Back then, just saying it aloud sent me into a downward spiral of emotions. Today, I can usually tell it like it's a story about somebody else without fully letting myself feel the emotions again. Honestly, it depends on where I am and why I'm telling my tale.

But since I didn't have cards printed, I've had to answer these questions over and over, starting with the ER triage nurse. So I stammered bluntly, "Both of the babies died," as tears began to roll down my cheeks. He stared at his screen while mumbling, "Sorry to hear that." This was the reply I would learn was standard fare when someone faces awkward silence. I got checked in and taken care of by a doctor, but it cemented my plan to avoid facing people as much as I possibly could.

Even when we did finally manage to go to the funeral home to pick up the babies' ashes and pick out urns, the workers there didn't know how to deal with us. To be frank, this wasn't the first time I sat in a funeral room office before, and I knew to expect their clichés and their forced, hushed expressions of sympathy. I knew that a funeral home was a business, and their motivation was to sell.

Clutching a blank check in my sweaty hands, I got out of the car with Brian and trudged past the perfectly manicured lawn into the foyer of the funeral home. Beads of sweat gathered around my temples, and Brian held my back to steady me. We entered, but there was no one to be seen, so we kept moving in, slowly.

"Oh, hello there, folks! How can I help you?" I turned to see a pudgy, smiling man puffing up the steps toward us.

"Hi. We are here to pick out two urns," I managed.

"Okay. Did you have an appointment?" He looked at his watch.

"No. We just . . . we just need to pick out the urns for our babies' ashes." It felt disgusting to even say it.

"Wait. What? Did you say babies? Hmm. Oh, well. Babies, then. Okay. So. Let me go check." He turned and shuffled back down the stairs, leaving us there to wait.

Minutes ticked by, and I realized that somewhere down those stairs they were probably playing rock, paper, scissors to see who had to come back up and deal with us. It could have even been that they were drawing straws or collecting on old favors owed. Whatever it was, it was taking forever.

When what seemed like an eternity had passed, and it felt like they were hoping that we would just leave, a woman walked up the same set of stairs with a huge, fake smile plastered on her face. "Are you the couple who lost a bayybeee?" she purred, tilting her head in our direction. "Let me take you and show you the most ADORABLE little Pooh Bear urns you have ever seen in your whole life. You are just going to love them! So cute, so cute. You just follow me now."

I wanted to punch this lady in the face. And *hard*. I wanted to run as fast as I could out of the door. I wanted to scream and pound my fists on the wall and whine and moan, and I wanted to go on television and tell the world that they didn't know the first thing about people grieving babies. I wanted to disappear.

Instead? Instead, we followed her to see the "adorable" urns. I choked back vomit while I paged through a catalog and tried to select the most peaceful looking ones I could find, wondering how you would know if an urn looked peaceful. After paging through, I finally decided on two tiny, mosaic-looking urns that looked calm and not at all "adorable." Pink for Sophie and blue for Aiden, just like the colors they would have worn when they came home from the hospital.

Once we were done there, grief rose up inside of me, threatening to spill over as I concentrated on just trying to make it to the car. Sitting down, I let it erupt, all of it, my tears spilling down my face, soaking my husband's shirt for what must have already been the thousandth time.

CHAPTER 5 - THEY WOULD HAVE BEEN SERIAL KILLERS

From: donotreply@store.com
Subject: Your friends and family are waiting for your registry!
Date: May 8, 2009
To: christywopat@email.com

We noticed your registry is empty! It's time to get acquainted with your Baby Registry. Begin by adding more of the items you love online, on your mobile phone, or in store. Get inspired with tips and advice from our tools and guides and share favorite finds with friends. And don't forget to pick up your free Baby Welcome Kit at your local store. It's our little gift to you.

"No, no, no. I want to *cancel* the registry. I don't want it anymore," I practically yelled into the phone.

"Well, ma'am," came the voice, "I'm looking at your baby registry now, and there is nothing on it. However, you will be getting a coupon soon to buy any more items you may need. I suggest putting more items on there so you can get a percentage off."

"Thank you, but I just need to delete it."

"Well, ma'am, you can do that by going to your registry online. I don't have the authority to delete it from where I am."

Tears of frustration started spilling as my voice cracked. "I *tried* to delete it. I need to cancel it. My . . . my babies died, and I keep getting coupons in the mail, and I just wish I could delete it, but it won't let me online, and this is the third call I've made."

"I do wish I could help, ma'am. I can transfer you over to our main hotline or your local store if you wish."

I hung up the phone, accepting defeat. The formula sample had pushed me over the edge. "Make sure your baby is getting ALL the nutrition he or she needs!" the flier had announced, making me slam my fist on the counter with frustration.

And now, on my third phone call, I still couldn't get anyone to delete the stupid thing. The prospect of getting coupons and fliers for my babies, the ones that were dead, was enough to make me want to never shop there again.

***

About five weeks after the twins died, we were lying in bed when Brian said to me, "So, babe . . . I kinda sorta don't want to bring something up that might make you upset. And, I know that I told you that all you needed to do was shower every day. But . . . are you ever planning on leaving the house again? I just don't want you to get that phobia where you can't even take fifteen steps outside the house to get the mail."

"Eff you," I scoffed. "Seriously. Where do you want me to go?"

As irritated as I was, however, after letting his words sink in, I supposed he had a point. Go get my hair cut. Go shopping. See my family. Those are things one *should* be doing.

Before any of that could happen, I would need to develop a plan. A procedure for what to do and what to say about the twins dying when I accidentally ran into someone I knew out and about. I *hated* telling people. Most of the time, I would say something like, "I delivered the twins at twenty-four weeks, but, sadly, they only lived for a day." And I would get, "Oh." Just that, or maybe, "Oh," along with a twisted-up face.

I daydreamed about making a loud buzzer that I could push after ridiculous responses, like the waah-waah sound when the person doesn't win the car on *The Price is Right.* "Nope. Sorry. That is not the correct response. Please try again."

Other times, the person might just stare at me, looking uncomfortable, which made *me* uncomfortable. So I would jump in and start apologizing for *their* discomfort. "No, please, don't worry about it. It's okay, I swear. It's fine." It was not fine.

I could never guess who was safe to tell because it honestly was never who I expected. If I told an older, wiser-looking woman, I might barely get a reply, even though I thought I'd get sympathy. On the other hand, I can remember finding kindness from the most unexpected of people. For the first Father's Day after the twins died, I went to the mall looking for a gift for Brian. I stopped at one of those kiosks where you can get things engraved and decided to buy a keychain with Aiden and Sophie's names on it. Of course, as I was filling out the order slip, tears were streaming down my face.

The teenage boy who was working asked gently, "Are you okay?"

I choked out, "These names . . . they . . . they are my babies that died."

He came out from behind the kiosk and awkwardly gave me a sideways hug. Then he said, "I'm only going to charge you cost for this. That totally sucks. You gave them nice names, though."

After this little talk with Brian, though, I woke up one morning, and I decided I was going to force myself to complete a project. Something to take my mind off the pain, to give me a purpose. Cleaning was out. Our house was on the market, so it was already pretty clean, and I didn't make much of a mess lying in bed all day anyway. I found going to the grocery store, or really out anywhere, to be complete and utter torture, so my husband took care of those errands, so those were out, too.

It was May in Wisconsin, and wet and gloomy spring days were dwindling, and we were getting more warm, sunny afternoons. One task we had been putting off was staining the wooden deck in our backyard.

After managing to take a shower, I pulled my hair back into a messy, wet bun, picked a loose-fitting, old T-shirt to hide my still-pregnant-looking belly, and headed out to the hardware store. After making it in without seeing anyone I knew, I quickly picked out three gallons of stain and a pack of brushes and headed home to get started.

Our house was a duplex on a quiet street in a small town. It was a starter home, something affordable for two young, just-married teachers so that we could build equity until we made enough to buy a bigger home. Our neighbors directly on the other side of our duplex were a young woman and her brother who were hardly ever home. Typically, we only saw her when she was mowing the lawn.

Directly behind our house, however, there was an older, retired couple. They took a walk nearly every night, and when they passed by, they would greet us or talk about the weather and make small talk. The wife adored our dog, so she would stop and give him a scratch behind the ears and ask us about the babies.

"Hi! Hello! Are you at home from work sick? What are you doing here? Is there a vacation day for the students?"

I looked up to see our elderly neighbor crossing the lawn toward my deck. My cheeks instantly flushed with *that* burn. That burn of knowing that something awful was about to happen. That burn of having to admit it, to say it out loud. I said, "No, I'm, uh . . . home on maternity leave."

Her eyes flashed down to my fleshy, still-rounded stomach. She looked me right in the eyes. I could see the wheels grinding in her mind; she was rolling this information around in there, trying to make sense of it.

"You had your twins, then? What in the world are you doing outside painting your deck? Where are the babies? Are they inside sleeping?"

I could see that she was looking around, probably for a baby monitor or something. Here she was, staring at a brand new "mother" staining her deck. She was still trying to make some sense of it, I suppose. I mean, seriously, what the hell kind of mother of newborn twins would be outside staining her deck, alone, with the door shut and no baby monitor?

I looked up at her, rising to my feet. "They . . . they were born. But, they died. They were sick and born early, and they died."

She looked down at her feet. I knew this made her uncomfortable. I was just too sad to try to save her. I wanted her to save me. I looked directly at her, daring her to say the right thing.

She opened her mouth, and then shut it. And then . . . she turned on her feet, dug one foot into the ground, and took off. Running. This seventy-something woman turned around, and as fast as she could go, she ran back into her house. She didn't even look back.

I stood there, stunned. "How dare she?" I thought. Angry tears welled up and spilled over. In those few weeks since the twins had been born, anytime I went out anywhere, I had wanted to run. Run from my sadness, run from my anger, run from my pain. The fact that she, this stranger, ran away filled me with rage. Why did *she* get to run away? Because of her discomfort? Who was the one dealing with the discomfort? *ME!* I screamed inside my head, *I'M THE ONE WHOSE BABIES DIED!*

That day, at that exact moment, it hit me. We are so afraid of grief and sadness that people can't even stand to say it aloud. It makes people so uncomfortable that sometimes they can't even muster up the awful cliché about God's plan, or that they are in a better place, or that overused anecdote that they "had a friend who had a miscarriage once." Grieving the loss of a baby is so taboo that it is actually easier to physically turn and run than it is to face the situation.

Looking back, I never really stopped to wonder if there was a reason why she ran away. Could she have suffered a similar loss? Could she have had her own battle with infertility? In my frame of mind, I just assumed she was a horrible person who couldn't handle it.

My husband and I still bring up this situation from time to time. To be honest, nowadays it makes me laugh until my ribs hurt when I really start to think about it. When I let myself give in to the absurdity of a grown woman, not just figuratively, but literally running away from an uncomfortable situation, it makes me laugh. Perhaps that's crazy. Perhaps I should be angry about it or sad about it. But laughter has always saved me, and I'm letting it save me now.

***

The first place Brian basically forced me to go that didn't involve my immediate family was to a work function. "It's a nice drive," he said. "In the sun."

And so we drove, and held hands, and stopped for ice cream. And we talked about safe things: our TV shows, our next vacation, our one annoying friend. Calm had settled over me by the time we arrived, and I thought, "See, you can do this, Christy. This is just life. It's not so hard."

The first thing one of our colleagues said to me was, "I'm so sorry to hear about your miscarriage." I looked down.

She continued, "You know, I wanted to tell you that I have a friend who had a miscarriage, and now she says she doesn't regret it, like, at all, because if she hadn't miscarried that baby, she wouldn't have her daughter now. So she's, like, actually grateful for it."

Oh, my word. Honestly, it was all I could do not to grab her and shake her. I'm sure there was some sort of sentiment in that, and that she actually meant well. And I'm sure her friend really meant that, too. But man, it was just not the right thing to say to me! And, if I'm completely truthful, seven years later, I still kind of hold that against her. I shouldn't, but I do.

Today, I would have a reply. Today, I would be able to calmly say,

"I'm so glad your friend has found peace with her loss. I actually didn't have a miscarriage, but I am so sorry for her loss." And then I would move on. It wouldn't ruin my day. It wouldn't even make me cry. Roll my eyes? Sure. Curse a little later as I told the story to my husband? You bet. At the time, though, something like that would stay with me for days. That is the impact words have. One little comment, even a well-meaning one, can cause anguish for days.

To be clear, I don't blame other people for not knowing the right thing to say. Do I think there is room for some to learn a little more tact, a slightly better way to word things? Well, sure, but this is not limited to grief. I guess what I'm saying is, I know most people mean well, but it still totally sucks.

***

Even before the babies died, people were using worn out clichés to try to comfort me. An acquaintance of ours was on staff at the hospital where I was admitted, and despite our insistence that we wanted no visitors, she stopped by. I was lying in the hospital bed, flipping channels through awful daytime television. I heard her voice coming down the hall and I . . . well, I closed my eyes and pretended to be asleep. Let's just say I wasn't a fan and had no patience to deal with her.

She opened with the perfunctory, "How *are* you?" along with a classic head tilt. Brian straightened up his shoulders, looked her in the eye, and replied with the ever-classic, "As good as can be expected, I guess." We actually got really good, really fast at answering annoying questions with something equally as annoying. Sometimes, it stopped people. Most of the time, not.

"Well, there will be other pregnancies, you know. She's still young." More head nodding.

I WAS STILL PREGNANT. I was still pregnant, both babies were still inside of me, and nobody really knew what was going to happen. The fact that she was assuming they would die felt like a hot poker in my eyeball. I started to feel guilty that Brian had to answer all of this nonsense on his own, but I couldn't bring myself to open my eyes and deal with it.

At that point, I couldn't and wouldn't accept that my babies were going to die. I truly kept believing that somehow it was going to be okay, that we were all going to be okay. I was dying on the inside, thinking about "other pregnancies." It had taken me so long just to get pregnant this time; how could I even think about doing that all over again?

Today, seven years later, we can pretty much laugh it off when we think about how absurd it was. I mean, it's ignorance and cruelty all wrapped up in one. How anyone could think that this was helpful is way beyond anything I could ever understand.

Was there anything worse than that? I can do worse. Yup.

"Honey, here's the deal. When *these things happen*, it's always *for a reason.* God knows what he is doing and you may not know why, but I bet you'll find out someday. I had a miscarriage in between my girls, and that was just not meant to be. Honestly. You know what? I bet those babies were going to grow up and be serial killers. God couldn't let that happen, so he ended it. The next pregnancy will be better. Just you wait." (That was a relative. I swear. I wish I was making this up.)

I guess there wasn't a lot you *could* say to me that would make me happy. Really, there was a way to turn anything that anyone said into something that just really, entirely, pissed me off. The one exception? "I'm sorry. That is so awful." That one worked just fine.

Since then, I've appointed myself "President of side-tracking people from saying stupid things to someone who is grieving." I follow sad people around and bust the kneecaps of known offenders. Okay, not really—but I really do try to look out for my fellow grievers and sufferers of infertility, especially online. I try to be the very first person to comment. And truthfully, whatever I write, everyone else after me writes their own little version of that same thing. Because who really knows what to say? Hardly anyone, unless you've been through it yourself, I'm pretty sure.

Now I absolutely realize that many of us do believe that life is not random and that there is a plan that has already been laid out for yours. I do not find fault in this belief—I know that this brings comfort to many people. But unless you know for sure that the person with whom you are speaking would be comforted by that, I would skip it, especially in the early days. Even when you do believe that God has a plan for you, it sometimes makes you really wonder why in the world your plan involves something as tragic as having your child die.

There are plenty of other things people say in an attempt to make you feel better when you are grieving. Some examples are:

He/she is in a better place now.

God needed another angel for His army.

You were his/her mother because God knew you were strong enough to handle it.

God doesn't give you more than you can handle.

For me, not a single one of these helped. In fact, hearing them would just make me angrier. It is so difficult because I would hear these things and come home, and I'd cry and wail to my husband. He is so level-headed, and he would always remind me that people are just doing their best. He would remind me that I needed to shake it off and be the bigger person. (Can you see how clichés made me want to poke my eyeballs out with a fork?!) I tried! I seriously tried. I never lost my cool with anyone, but in my head I would be screaming the answers to all those platitudes.

The only place they should be is right here with me!

That doesn't even make any sense!

I am so, so totally not strong enough to handle this!

Then He obviously has no idea what people can or cannot handle!

Intention really does matter, and so I was always grateful for people who tried to comfort me, even if it wasn't exactly what I needed to hear. People were doing their best, but I found myself pulling away from them anyway.

I started to develop social anxiety because I just knew that whenever I saw someone, I would spend the entire conversation worrying about what they were going to say. Even strangers who didn't know me would sometimes bring up questions that I didn't want to answer. When you really think about it, small talk is brutal for someone who is grieving a recent loss. Whether it's a stranger who is asking "get to know you" type questions (How many kids do you have?), or someone you know who didn't hear the news (Where are the twins?), it's painful. This can absolutely cause roadblocks in healing and in mental health, especially if you begin going to extreme measures to avoid these situations.

Quite often I get asked for advice about how to comfort someone who has lost a child. Getting out of the early years of grief has allowed me to really analyze my experiences, and I have found that people really do want to know what to do. And really, would I know all of this if I hadn't lived through it? Definitely not. I'd like to think I was always an empathetic person, but I'm sure I used the general "It'll be okay. Everything will be alright," with someone in pain.

I really, truly, can't speak for everyone because we are all so different. As I said earlier, especially in the raw, early days of grief, using broad religious or faith-based replies typically doesn't help, even when the person is strong in his or her faith. For example, saying, "God has a plan for you" would, in my experience, not be comforting in those early days; however, posting a specific Bible verse that would provide advice or solace would absolutely be appropriate.

Trying to explain why a tragedy happens is futile. In the end, it doesn't matter *why* it happened, it just matters that it happened. We try so hard to assign blame or responsibility, but it cannot bring the person back. Grieving people are in so much pain, and unfortunately, there just isn't a lot to say that can actually help.

There are a lot of things you can *do*, however. Instead of trying to make them feel better, simply let them know you are there. Hold her hand and hug her. Tell him you know things suck really bad right now and ask if he wants to play basketball. Instead of saying, "I'm here for whatever you need," say, "I'm leaving a lasagna on your porch at four. Will you be home?"

Ask, point blank, if something helps or doesn't help. Hardly anyone really asked me, but after a while, I just came out and told people what I needed. I like to see my babies' names. I like to know that they are remembered. A text on their birthday. A "like" on my post about how I'm thinking about them.

My friends and family know that I like to hear Sophie and Aiden's names. I have a friend who would rather not. Seeing her baby's name is too painful, and she does not find comfort in that. The only thing you can do to avoid causing pain is to ask questions. Be there. Tell them you know it sucks.

And, please, do not tell them their baby would have been a serial killer.

CHAPTER 6 - LIGHTEN UP

http://lacrosse.craigslist.org

Baby Furniture for Sale(LaCrosse)

I have two brand-new baby cribs for sale, along with two glider rockers and a matching changing table. Brand-new mattresses as well.

Cash only. You haul. We are in Onalaska.

To: h5m3f-5538096175@sale.craigslist.org
RE: Baby Furniture for Sale

Hello, I don't need your baby furniture, but I just wanted to write you and say that I am so sorry for your loss. I am praying for you and your family.
Sincerely,
Rebecca

To: h5m3f-5538096175@sale.craigslist.org
RE: Baby Furniture for Sale

hi can u cut me a deal im having twins and they r sooooo much money

It wasn't long after we got home from the hospital that the flashbacks began. Lying down in bed, I would roll onto my side, burrow into my pillow, and be instantly transported back in time. It was almost as if I could hear the actual "pop!" and then the moment would swallow me up whole. Lying there, I would silently weep while my husband attempted to comfort me. I struggled to get myself out of the moment, out of the trauma itself. Oftentimes the only thing I could do was to close my eyes and replay that entire night from start to finish. Stopping was impossible until I finished playing the entire story out in my head like a movie.

If I ever found myself in bed at exactly 9:40 p.m., I would totally freak out. Do you remember how that night, after I felt the "pop" of my water breaking, I happened to look up at the clock and notice it said 9:40? Well, for the next two weeks that I was still pregnant, Brian and I had a ritual that each night at 9:41 p.m. we would scratch off a lottery ticket to celebrate that we were twenty-four hours closer to the age of viability. They were those stupid $2 crossword puzzle tickets that you scratched off one letter at a time until you figured out there was no way you were going to win. For us, though, winning was making it another day, another step closer to our little babies coming home.

Turns out they weren't ever coming home, and so that time became a daily punch in the gut, a giant "Fuck You" every twenty-four hours.

The first thing I figured out was that taking the clock down from the wall helped a little. If I didn't know what time it was, I couldn't panic about it, right? It started there, rather innocently. After that, I went online and ordered a brand new comforter, pillows, and soft sheets. Paint was next. A gray to match the new comforter, of course, and I begged my husband to help me rearrange our heavy bedroom furniture.

It worked for a while, but it was never enough. I would feel temporarily satisfied with the change, but soon it would lose its novelty, and something else would pop up that was distressing. Worse, there was a permanently closed door in our hallway—one that I had not opened since we arrived home empty-handed. Brian and I never spoke about it. We knew what was in there, we knew we would have to deal with it, but we chose not to right away. I know some families who left the nursery exactly the same, gathering dust, for years and years. Others took things down immediately. My mother's mother took hers down for her before she even arrived home from the hospital after my sister was born still. For what it's worth, I don't think there's a "right" timeline for this.

My next idea was to start planning a different, better escape route. Spontaneous, random trip to France, just the two of us? Sure! Why not? We were both teaching French at the time, and if there's any place in the world we love the most, it's Paris! Without really having the money, we booked a trip to France for just the two of us. Throwing myself into planning, we arranged for a hotel in the heart of Paris and began dreaming up what we would do. We'd walk along the Seine, hand in hand, eating pain au chocolat and listening to street musicians. We'd sit in the Jardin du Luxembourg until the sun went down and watch the Eiffel Tower sparkle with her beautiful lights. We'd skip the other major monuments we'd already seen, and we'd *really* see Paris. The dreams piled up like presents under the Christmas tree, and I became fixated on making it perfect.

In the meantime, I began slowly trying to convince Brian that we should sell our house. We were practically newlyweds; we hadn't even lived in our house for three years. But it wasn't really a practical time to sell—we had put zero percent down and were on the very tip of the iceberg when it came to payments. None of this really troubled me (I have always believed that happiness trumps money, which explains why my credit card statement was much higher before I got married!), but Brian is extremely money-conscious, and he knew the market was terrible. He said, "I totally get why you want to move, babe, but we're talking about losing thousands of dollars here. I just don't think we can . . ."

But, I begged. I pleaded. I was convinced that we *deserved* a fresh start. That it was time to make new memories and get away from the bad ones. Brian was still hesitant, but I managed to persuade him to have a realtor come over and give us an idea about possibly selling our house. All we'd ask for was an estimate. I called someone right away.

The morning of the appointment, I woke with a glimmer of excitement. These feelings were few and far between, so I gave in and started letting myself get hopeful. I lit candles and fluffed pillows, and I felt a sense of pride as I noticed the changes we made to our house in preparation. About thirty minutes before the realtor was set to arrive, I walked upstairs to do a final check of the top level. Walking down the hallway, I paused in front of the nursery. I took a deep breath and turned the doorknob . . . and walked in.

My senses were overwhelmed, and I immediately regretted entering. Time had frozen inside that room, as if we had run out for milk one night and never returned. Coincidentally, the night before my water broke was the night that Brian decided to put the cribs together. The drill was still sitting on the floor, as if in mid-use. I ordered those gorgeous cribs just as soon as our twenty-week ultrasound had a great report. Looking back, I had been very cautious when I hadn't really had a reason to be. I was always, always worried about something going wrong, but I couldn't really say why. Yes, my mom had lost a baby, but I didn't know the details of that, and I figured that used to happen a lot a long time ago. I remember calling a friend while I waited in the hospital lobby, telling her I was so nervous for the ultrasound. "For heaven's sake, what are you worried about?" she replied.

The cribs were in there, along with two glider-rockers. There were tiny pink and blue outfits hanging in the closet. The walls were freshly painted a mint green—neutral, since we were having a boy and a girl. A mound of expensive diaper boxes sat in the closet since I thought it would be a good idea to buy them a few at a time leading up to the birth.

As I stared, my heart started to pound. The realtor. The realtor would look in this room. What the hell had I been thinking? I began to sweat. "Focus, Christy," I told myself. I needed a plan, and I needed it quickly. For a second, a pathetic second, I wondered if I could just say I was pregnant with twins. After all, I had been. And I still looked pregnant enough.

I started to lose my breath and backed out of the room into my bedroom. I really didn't know it then, but it was the beginning of perpetual panic attacks. Next to me on my nightstand sat a book. It was one of the only books about grief that I had been able to find at the library, and the title was clear enough that you could easily tell it was about the loss of a baby. I grabbed the book and went across the hall and eased the door open again. I figured if he did indeed go in there, I would just need to set the book somewhere so he could see it, and then he just wouldn't say anything. I looked around and carefully balanced the book on the corner of the first crib, the one right next to the door.

Later, as the realtor looked around downstairs, all I could focus on was where he was inevitably headed, and I repeated a command in my head as if willing it would make it happen. "Don't go upstairs. Don't go upstairs."

He nodded that he had seen enough and then noticed the stairs.

"The bedrooms are up there?" he asked.

"Uh, yes, but they're just normal bedrooms. On the small side, nothing really exciting," I stammered back. But he turned and headed up the stairs. For a moment I contemplated following him, but decided I was safer just waiting for him downstairs. He paused at the bottom.

"Will you lead the way?"

He looked in all of the other rooms first and then stopped at the nursery. He turned the knob, opened the door, looked in, and then closed the door and looked at me. He chewed on his pen, tapping the clipboard against his leg in a weird kind of *tap, tap, tap* pattern.

"So," he said, "you guys, like, trying to have a bunch of kids or something?" he asked, and then kind of chuckled.

"Um, yeah," I answered. "Something like that."

We did end up putting our house on the market after the realtor assured us we would at the very least break even and not lose money. In the meantime, we began a ritual to go and look at open houses. It was a great distraction, and when we were looking I could pretend to be anyone I wanted to be. Every Sunday like clockwork, we would get dressed, grab the newspaper, and head out to as many open houses as we could find. We'd make notes about what we liked or didn't like; we'd look at houses that were total dumps and ones that we could never afford in a million years. Brian even made a spreadsheet for us to keep track of everything. Sometimes we would find one that we would want to see again, and we'd ask our realtor to get us an appointment to look.

Our realtor was a strange man. He dressed in the same button-down, Hawaiian print shirt and cargo shorts every single time we met, and he had a really annoying laugh. He chewed his fingernails and breathed really heavily and told us weird things like he had once painted eyeballs on his son's ceiling. He said things like, "Oh, I seen that the other day," and "supposably." He worked for a real estate business that offered a discount. One flat fee, no matter how much the house cost, instead of a percentage. He would pick us up in his big, loud Ford truck and drive us from house to house.

One day, we went to look at a house that was for sale by owner. When we arrived, the owners were still home, and I tensed up immediately when I saw the woman was very, very pregnant. I looked at my husband, trying to tell him with my eyes that I wanted out. He squeezed my hand and then gripped my elbow and whispered in my ear, "We'll make this one quick."

I hated looking at houses with baby nurseries. It made me despise myself because I was so jealous and angry and, honestly, borderline hateful. On this day, the woman was walking us around her house, with her perfect, eight-month pregnant belly. *At least thirty-two weeks,* I thought. *Even if her baby was born today, he'd be fine with a little NICU time.* She led us to the top of a staircase, stopped, and turned toward us.

"I see you don't have any children with you. Do you have any? Because the reason we're trying to move is that there is only one bedroom upstairs. So we have to put the nursery downstairs. That is not ideal, ya know? And there is *no* way that my husband will let this baby sleep in our room, so, yeah. We need to move. And this baby will hopefully get here quickly because I am *so* over being pregnant. I mean, have you seen my ankles?"

I stood there, the pain and the anger and the jealousy and just downright rage battering my heart like a hurricane. I watched her going down the stairs, holding onto her belly, and I muttered under my breath, "Gee. Wouldn't it be a shame if she fell." And I made a kicking motion with my foot. And I giggled. I *giggled*.

The realtor and my husband both stopped dead in their tracks and turned to look at me. The realization of what I had just said sort of kicked in, but I want to be honest here—I just didn't care. I had been broken into a million little pieces. The pain was so strong that, while I definitely did *not* mean it—there is no way I would ever want to hurt someone or see someone hurt—in my mind, I just felt like I had a right to feel this way.

Losing my babies gave me the right to be a total bitch and do what I wanted and say what I wanted, and everybody else should just have to understand. Whenever I was upset, I deserved to be mad and that person should apologize. Grief can cause you to be so selfish, although I would say deservedly so.

It also made me believe that everyone else's life was picture-perfect, and that it was totally unfair that mine was not. In some ways, and this is extremely difficult to admit, I just felt like everyone else should have to suffer, too.

I pushed past the two men as I headed down the stairs, saying, "God, I was just kidding. Lighten up."

***

Nothing made me ready to take that nursery down. It sounds ridiculous because I knew Aiden and Sophie were dead, but having that room full of their things (Were they really theirs? They had never even been in them), felt like a betrayal to them. It felt like admitting it was really over. The other thing, and this feels difficult to say now, is that I was convinced I'd have twins again, and then everything would be okay.

I know. I know this sounds hypocritical because if anyone said anything to me like, "You are young, and there will be other babies, and everything is going to be okay," I would have finished the conversation, gone home and screamed and wailed and declared that NO ONE UNDERSTOOD ME OR MY GRIEF. But then, here I am admitting that I really thought I'd have another set of twins, and then everything would be okay. That my life would be back on track, fixed somehow.

It was a compulsion. Being a twin mom was something that I was *so* proud of. It felt like something that made everything extra special, extra exciting. To go from infertile to instant family was an incredible, life-changing miracle. I had already subscribed to the online club, *Moms of Multiples*, found a twin-mom group in the area, and found out which children's clothing stores would give you a discount if you bought two of the same item. Deep down, I knew it was never going to happen now. Getting pregnant with twins again was something that would have to be avoided at all costs, for my health and for the health of the babies.

That didn't stop me from dreaming and planning, though. And each time we decided to sell the cribs, I would decide not to because . . . what if? And then I would swing back to absolutely without-a-doubt needing to get those things out of my house forever so I would never have to look at them again.

And so, eventually, we put them on Craigslist, not knowing what kind of shit storm that would create. I had sold a zillion things on the site before with hardly any issues, but all of a sudden, it was personal. I was getting emails blatantly asking why I was selling two brand-new cribs. Others accused me of lying so I could sucker them into paying more money. Yet others weren't interested in the furniture at all, but rather wanted to send me well-wishes because they had assumed the worst.

You have no idea how I wished I didn't need the money from the sale, and I could just get rid of it all. I wanted to throw each piece of furniture out of the window. I wanted never to see or touch or think about it again. A theme began to emerge, and once it all finally sold, I went on a rampage, wanting to rid my house of any evidence of twin existence. I chose one plastic tub, and in it I saved the first outfits we bought for them, a pair of pink and blue booties that someone had knitted for us, and the prayer blankets someone had given us from their church. I wrote the word TWINS on it in black marker and had Brian put it in the garage where I couldn't see it unless I asked for it.

We never did end up taking that trip to Paris. Reality got in the way, as it so typically does, and it just wasn't happening for us. We used the airline credits to fly to Las Vegas instead, just to be somewhere else on the twins' due date. Planning for it gave me a tiny purpose and helped keep me from going off the rails during that time period. It got me out of bed each day, quite literally.

***

Soon, though, I just had to swallow the fact that none of this was enough. Nothing I was doing was taking away any of the pain, the longing, the deep, dark ache for a baby. Whether I was obsessively and compulsively cleaning and organizing my house, or throwing myself into a project, or creating something as a memorial to the babies, nothing worked. I'm pretty sure that this is the point in the grieving process when people start drinking, doing drugs, and/or cheating on their spouses.

After experiencing what grief can do to the heart and soul, I now totally and completely understand and empathize with how someone can completely lose control. And I'm guessing it would probably make for a better, juicier book if I had started on a bender or needed to go to rehab or had a tragic love affair with my husband's brother (he doesn't have one, so that would have been on the more difficult side).

Well, I didn't.

The truth is, I've never been a drinker. As in, we don't even drink socially at dinner with friends. I understand that others don't think this is normal. People look at us funny when we order. Assume I'm pregnant when I say 'no thanks.' Probably assume we are recovering alcoholics who need to stay sober. Really, we just don't like the way it makes us feel and how much it costs. But even with us never, ever drinking, I could feel the pull. The desire to numb the pain for even a few minutes was strong. Stronger than anything I'd felt before.

I would sit and wonder how good it would feel to smoke marijuana. I would contemplate a bottle of tequila or a bottle of white wine. I was lazy and depressed and didn't want to leave my house, though, and Brian wouldn't buy it for me. (Love you, babe! Thanks again for that!)

I did, however, medicate with food, my typical drug of choice. Frequent trips to fast food restaurant drive-thrus, devouring bags of chips and giant diet sodas in the Big Gulp size—all of it felt pretty good. I hardly cooked any sort of meal and didn't care a single iota about what was going in my mouth. I don't remember if this bothered my husband or not, but if it did, he didn't say anything.

I was absolutely, positively, no fun to be around. I was sarcastic to the point of being what you might call a bitch. Bitter and jealous and sad. So, so sad. We canceled plans a lot, and the things we did attend resulted in me getting upset, almost inevitably. We went to fireworks for the Fourth of July that year and once they started, I sat in my chair, sobbing, wishing I could be swallowed by a great chasm that ate up the soccer field and everyone in it.

It was do or die time. I could almost feel myself slipping away into the dark feelings. I was grumpy more than I was cheerful, depressed more than I was happy. I was one of those people who felt like taking medication was giving up, admitting I couldn't handle it. Luckily, I realized that it wasn't giving up at all—it was time to get help.

CHAPTER 7 - WELL, THAT WAS SUPER FUN

In the "Bereaved Parents" folder we got from the hospital, there was a brochure with the ever-famous "dew-drop leaf" picture that provided information about a grief group. It met once a month for a few hours. This was way, *way* out of Brian's comfort zone, but he agreed that it seemed like something important for us to at least try. As you have probably already realized, I am lucky to have Brian as my husband.

The meeting took place in the basement of the main hospital campus. One long hallway after another, we followed signs that read "Infant Loss Support Group This Way" until we reached a small, closed-off, dark room. A young couple sat uncomfortably wedged together on a too-small loveseat, and next to them a middle-aged woman slowly rocked back and forth in a hard wooden chair with her hands clasped together in her lap. After awkward greetings, we found seats on a couch adjacent to the counselor, a woman who looked to be in her sixties and had kind eyes. Her name was Jan.

Jan opened with, "Well, I am so glad to see you here tonight. I am also very sorry to see you here tonight because that means you have suffered an exceptional loss. Let's start with introductions. Please tell us your names, what kind of infant loss you experienced, and how long ago your loss happened."

The couple went first. They spoke slowly, robotically, like they were reading off of a teleprompter. "Seven weeks ago we had a stillborn child at thirty-two weeks. We went to a routine exam and found out there was no heartbeat. We induced delivery, and our daughter was born."

Next to them, the woman began with her name and then said, "My baby boy was born at full-term a year and a half ago and had a genetic heart defect. He didn't survive."

All eyes turned to me, and my heart began to beat faster. Tears welled up, and I wondered how these women were able to say it with such ease—or so it seemed. How was it that they could just say, point blank, "My baby is dead" and not even blink? My words came out in a blur, strung together in a semi-coherent sentence. "My name is Christy, and I had two babies, and they were born early, and they were sick, and they lived in the hospital, but they both died."

Even today, it is difficult for me to summarize this in one sentence. Sometimes I still cry when I say it. This is something that I want, and need, for people to know about me, but I wish they could just already know it without me having to tell them. People's varied reactions are still a mystery to me. In this situation, I knew that there would be sympathy, but it's in my character to over-analyze everything. Would they think my loss was not as bad because they were born so early? Did they hear the part that Aiden and Sophie had lived for a brief time?

"Okay, so next let's talk about the hardest thing that we faced since we met last. Tell us what it was, and why it was difficult. Who would like to start?"

Without missing a beat, one woman spoke up. "My family doesn't understand why I am still pumping my breast milk. It's not very much anymore, but what is there I take out to my daughter's grave, and I let it spill all over." Her eyes met mine as she explained. "Pumping is stopping me from drying up, and I feel like I still want to feed her. Since I couldn't." Tears spilled from her eyes as her husband placed his hand on her thigh, making jerky, almost violent circles there. "I don't want anyone to know, but sometimes it gets painful, and I have to do it, and they find out."

My eyes looked to the floor, my head swimming. *This lady is crazy*, I thought. *I'm not as crazy as she is! I must not need therapy! Time to go home! Peace out, yo!*

So, I was not ready for group therapy. I was still in denial. That sweet, grieving woman, whose name I cannot remember, was absolutely not even close to being "crazy." My breasts only partially filled up with breast milk. They hurt for a day or two and then pretty much dried up. Since that meeting, I've met women who donated their breast milk for months after their loss, who squeezed it out and spread it on a grave or a tree or flowers. But at the time, even as someone who could understand the pain, I judged her for it.

She went on to describe how a family member had sent her a nasty email because she posted a picture online of giving her baby a bath in the hospital after she was born. "You're making everyone uncomfortable," the email read. "It's too morbid."

My initial reaction was to be flabbergasted. And then guilty. Ashamed, really. I flashed back to being in the NICU, awkwardly holding my babies, worried about doing it right, trying not to break them even though they were already dead. I didn't even know how to hold my babies, and she had bathed and dressed hers. What kind of a mom was I?

Death is ugly. With few exceptions, we don't like to think about dead bodies and what they look like. Some of us don't want to talk about it at all. Others are fascinated by it, or even specialize in it. When my babies each took their last little gasps in my arms, I was not prepared for how they would look. How quickly they would change from alive to dead. After Aiden died, a nurse asked if I would like pictures taken with my twins together.

"How is that even possible?" I had asked. "Sophie died yesterday."

She replied, "Honey. I'll go get her. She's just downstairs. You'll want pictures with them together."

"No!" I half-shouted. "Leave her alone. Leave her where she is."

As it turns out, the nurse did go back to the morgue and get Sophie. She took her from the cold drawer where she was being kept and placed her next to her brother, next to the baby whom she had always been right next to, until I delivered her way too early.

This still stings. I understand that the nurse thought she knew better. I understand that she didn't want me to make a decision I would someday regret. I am not angry with her, really, because I think I know why she did it. And my fellow bereaved mamas have all sorts of different experiences with their babies after they died, ranging from bathing and dressing their baby, to having the baby sleep in their hospital room, to even taking the baby home so he or she can sleep in a treasured crib.

I was more on the other end of the spectrum. I wanted them, my tiny little, perfectly formed babies, to rest. I didn't want to think about them being in a drawer in a cold morgue. And those pictures now remind me that that's where they were. And that the only pictures I will ever have of them together show them to be very . . . dead. There is really no other way to describe it.

I have never put those photographs on social media. Many times I have wanted to. Almost even been desperate to. "Sorry about your miscarriage; I had one too," someone would inevitably say, and I had this longing for people to understand that I did *not* have a miscarriage. But the truth is, unless you've lived through it, you can't really understand. You can have sympathy, and you can care, and you can ask questions, but you can't feel what I felt and still feel. And that's okay. Actually, that's good. I wouldn't wish this pain on anyone in the world. Back then? I may have wanted to, in my fog of grief, just for a moment. Mostly just because I needed validation, for someone to say, "Oh my gosh, what you are going through must be the worst thing ever. I am so sorry."

As we got in the car that night after the support group, Brian said, "Well, that was super fun," and a wave of adoration for him came over me. "I planned my escape route sixteen different ways," I said. "I was ready to say I had severe explosive diarrhea, but she finally told us it was over." With a chuckle, the conversation turned to a book I was reading, and we never went back or spoke about it again.

It wasn't for us. That particular group wasn't. I truly think we just weren't mentally ready. If we had waited and then gone a few weeks later, I bet we would've loved it. Sometimes it's a matter of when. Sometimes it's a matter of who. It is so important to feel like you click with people in order to share your story.

Not long after that support group, I read a book that talked about the high rate of divorce that comes along with infant/child loss. The statistics were startling. I looked carefully at Brian, measuring up our chances. We had been married for less than three years, and during that time we had watched his dad fight and die from lung cancer, then the two years of negative pregnancy tests, and now this. How did our chances stack up? Someone recently asked me why I thought we were able to stay together. I attribute it to a few things. First, I don't think we love each other more than any other married couple. Our marriage was new, and it hadn't been easy. My guess is that since I did a lot of research about how to heal, it helped. That being said, I'm sure that luck had a little bit to do with it, too. I found out right away that a loss like this could completely derail your marriage. Then I read an entire book written by a psychologist that talked about how men and women grieve differently.

And, boy, they really do, in my experience. Initially, I harbored resentment for Brian. I resented him because he didn't seem to want to talk about it, he wasn't crying, and because he hadn't held either of the babies. Back then, I couldn't understand why he hadn't done those things, and it had made me feel so alone, and sometimes even stupid for being as sad as I was. I didn't have the courage or emotional strength to even really talk to him about it, and it didn't take too long before things started to fester.

It's funny because in the thick of my grief, in the worst moments, even I would doubt myself. The uncertainty would seep in, curling its tendrils around my thoughts like smoke from a fire. *Why are you so sad, you dumb girl? You didn't even know them! They were here for a minute, and then they weren't!* I'd think that Brian was right, and that he didn't seem so sad because there wasn't really anything to be all that sad about. *Get over it, Christy! Buck up!*

Other people thought that, too. I know they did. Maybe even still do. Not too long ago I heard someone in the teachers' lounge speaking about her grandpa who had died before she was born. "I don't miss him," she'd said. "How can you miss someone you never even knew?"

Still, I worried that the repercussions of *not* grieving "the right way" would be harmful, so I called and made us an appointment with a counselor. I couldn't let go of the fact that everyone, everywhere, was telling us we needed someone else to help us heal. We decided to each do our own hour separately so we could be honest without hurting the other person.

The office was in a larger wing of one of the local hospitals. I was met by a puff of stale air as I walked in with Brian close behind. An older woman with curly dark hair greeted me as she continued to type on her computer. "You can go ahead and sit down," she said, as she pointed to a line of mismatched chairs along the wall. Brian and I shuffled over and sat, immediately reaching for each other.

Although it was just us and the receptionist in the waiting room, it seemed chaotic. There were decade-old magazines on a side table and outdated fliers haphazardly pinned to a bulletin board. I remember one flier said something like, "If you've ever wondered what difference a week can make, ask the mom of a premature baby."

A week. One week and my babies would probably be alive. One week may have been the difference between life and death. That sign made me think that maybe, just maybe, this counselor would understand me, though, and I calmed a little.

The door opened, and a patient, an older gentleman, walked out with his head down. He made a uncomfortable beeline for the exit, and we stood. The counselor held out her hand and said, "Hello, there. You must be Christy." I shook her hand lightly and followed her into her office.

Matching the chaos of the outside, her office was also a mixture of clutter and yellowing paperwork. I remember wondering if I'd have to lay on a couch like they do on TV. You know, get comfortable and share my deepest, darkest secrets. But there was no couch here, and there were hardly even any comfortable-looking chairs.

"So, Christy, tell me why you're here," she directed, looking me in the eye. I looked down. I always looked down. In those early days, I couldn't face anyone. I shifted in my chair, uncomfortable.

I could have told her, "I had twins that were born at twenty-four weeks, and they didn't survive." Those are the facts. But why was I seeking help? That's a whole different story. The 'why' is so much more difficult to put into words than the facts.

I don't actually remember what I told her. I just remember beginning to cry and not being able to communicate very clearly. So much was wrong. My life felt . . . over. The despair was so overwhelming that putting it into words was impossible.

By the end of that first appointment, I had a diagnosis: post-traumatic stress disorder, or PTSD. Not shocking, I suppose. I was reliving the events over and over, I was avoiding anything and everything that would remind me of it, and I had pretty much only negative feelings about myself and my life. The worst of it was how irritable I felt all the time, and how angry. I couldn't sleep, I couldn't concentrate, I couldn't read a book or complete a task without difficulty.

Her plan was to do something with me called Eye Movement Desensitization and Reprocessing (EMDR). As it was being explained to me, though, I was totally thinking that it was wacky. It involved unpacking my terrible experiences, desensitizing myself to them— using tapping, which I thought was *so* weird—and teaching myself not to have a physical reaction to the bad memories.

I went every week, religiously, and did exactly what the therapist asked of me. I pictured my "happy spot," which was the place that made me feel calm. Even though my grandmother passed away years and years ago, thinking about sitting at her kitchen table was the happiest place that came to mind.

My job was to tell my story, starting from the beginning. And when I started to feel anxious, I had to tap my forehead and think of sitting at my grandma's table. Another strategy I learned was that when a memory was bugging me, I should close my eyes and make an image in my mind of that memory being locked up in a treasure chest. Then I should wrap a chain around it. And then dump it in the ocean and picture it sinking all the way to the bottom.

I think I continued for about eight or ten sessions, and I liked it more and more each time. After that, I knew that I had gotten all I could get out of it, and I stopped going. I can't lie, so I should say that part of the reason I stopped was that it was very expensive, and my insurance didn't cover it. I think if it had been covered, I would have at least finished the entire cycle of EMDR. But overall, I was glad I went, and I was glad I had someone to talk to. It helped to calm my swirling and stormy thoughts. It's so important that you try things and figure out what is going to work for you.

For me, writing was my biggest savior. Writing was how I healed. But everyone will find their own path to healing. Some of my blog friends absolutely loved their therapists. Some weren't comfortable with that and visited support groups instead. Others healed through service to the church or starting their own fundraisers or foundations.

The most important thing for me to remember was that whatever was working for me was the right thing for me. If you are in the depths of this pain right now, don't worry about whether or not you're doing the "right" thing. Find what works for you and hang on for dear life!

CHAPTER 8 - THE INTERNET SAVED MY LIFE

From: christy@email.com
Subject: DUDE.
Date: May 20, 2009
To: bree@email.com

OK, seriously. Tell me I don't suck and that I am not the worst person EVER! But, I was just at Target . . . I just needed to get out and try to feel normal. It was my first time going in months. Anyway, I walked in and right away I started getting really dizzy. I swear, EVERYWHERE I looked there were pregnant people. Honestly, even when I was dealing with infertility BS, I didn't notice all the pregnant chicks out there!

I don't know what made me do it, I swear I'm such a moron, but I started looking in the baby section. Stupid Target won't take me off the registry list even though I've called 3 times and I had this idea that I could just go and add more stuff to it. You know . . . for next time. I don't know WHAT I was thinking. Anyway . . . I was back there and this girl was next to me with her stupid huge belly and perfect hair and she was all, "When are you due? I just had my shower but I still need like 8 million things and so I'm here any chance I can get!"

Bree, she sounded so . . . freaking HAPPY and I'm telling you . . . I wanted to punch her. I really think I might have. I just wanted to punch the smug, "Look at how perfect I am" look right off her stupid face.

But, guess what I did?

I said, "I still have a while. I'm having twins, so I need two of everything, you know."

And then I rounded the corner, left my cart piled with crap in the aisle, and ran to my car and cried for 25 minutes.

My life = pile of shit.

From: bree@email.com
To: christy@email.com

You are so not the worst person ever. You don't suck. All I can think about is being pregnant again. Seriously. It's all I can think about. My husband is researching the different kinds of cerclages available. We'll have a baby someday! Promise!

Xoxo
Bree

From: christy@email.com
To: bree@email.com

OK . . . but promise me that if I can't, you'll help me steal one?

Xoxo
Christy

Before Brian left for his first day back at work, he told me, "I don't care what you do—watch TV, read books, sleep, whatever—but promise me you'll get up every single day and take a shower. Do it for you." I cannot even begin to express what great advice that was.

He had been so kind and loving and strong for me—and so whatever he wanted me to do, I wanted to do it. I'd like to say that I used my time wisely and started a new hobby or had dinner waiting on the table every single night, but that would be too far from the truth. I slept a lot. Like, a lot, a lot. I watched TV. And I scoured the internet.

The internet saved my life. I wasn't suicidal if that's what you're thinking. Admittedly, in the early, dark days, I often wished that I could be dead instead of the twins or be dead so that I could be with them, but I never thought about actually dying or planned out ways to do it. But it saved me in so many ways. It must have been the second or third day that I was home alone. I pulled out my laptop, and into the search bar I typed, "I lost my twins."

The first thing I found was an article about miscarriage. My first thought was to keep scrolling because I didn't have a miscarriage. I clicked anyway, and as I read, my muscles tensed and my hands started to shake. Earlier that day, someone had sent me a card. It said, "Sorry about your miscarriage."

The anger came from a place of desperation to be understood. Damn it, people should have understood how much worse my pain was because my babies had been *alive*; they had been carried by me, *birthed by me*. I had gone through labor and delivery, and I had held them in my arms while they took their last breath. That was MUCH worse than a miscarriage, in my mind. I wanted them—everybody— to know how awful it was.

I have since heard this type of feeling dubbed the "Pain Olympics," and when you're in the thick of grief, you are a champion player. Of course, I know now that nothing is ever really as simple as "Mine is worse than yours." It wasn't long until I realized that other people thought it was more painful to lose a full-term baby than a preemie. They thought it was more painful to lose a five-year-old than an infant.

People started throwing out the phrase, "At least," to me. "At least you didn't lose the babies after you got to know them." "At least it wasn't like what happened to my cousin's/uncle's/friend's sister—they lost a toddler/high schooler." But when I said that miscarriage wasn't "as bad" as what I experienced, I was doing the same thing to miscarriage sufferers as people were doing to me—I was minimizing them. I was putting their pain on a scale based on my opinions or observations, and that wasn't fair.

I have come to the conclusion that there is no way to measure grief. I have met and gotten to know hundreds of women over the last few years, many of whom have stories very similar to mine, but we *all* have a different grief journey. Sure, we find many things in common, such as things that bother us or things that people have said to us, but our feelings are all unique. We all move through the stages of grief at varying speeds, and the decisions we make about how to cope with our grief are all different. We have varying degrees of faith, support, and resources; all of that plays a part. Even our ages or how many kids we already had or how many kids we wanted—these factors all determine what we think and feel.

If I had to choose the one thing from all of this that has made me better—a better friend, mother, daughter, wife, sister, colleague—it's the knowledge that someone else's pain is never yours to judge. I mean, okay, we all have the coworker who can find something to complain about no matter what, and the friend who gets really worked up about the tiniest of things. But I find that, in general, people are experiencing genuine pain, even if it doesn't seem to us like they should be. Truthfully, this life that we live is full of so many things that cause us pain and suffering, and we all just need someone to listen to us and say, "That really sucks. I am so sorry that's happening."

It was hard for me to let people know how horrific the experience was for me, and it continues to be difficult for me not to say aloud the "At least . . ." that pops into my head when someone is complaining about something. But, like most things, it has faded. The sharp edges of anger have dulled, and I have finally arrived at a place where I don't need people to feel sorry for me. I don't worry so much about people thinking I'm too sad or that I'm not moving on. I have less to prove. (But I still hate it when someone says "At least.")

After reading the article about miscarriage, I randomly came across a link that led me to a blog. I wasn't too familiar with what blogs were at the time (Do I really want to read an online diary about someone's day?), but it looked interesting. In the first entry that I read, the writer was describing a phone call from her mother that had left her gutted and sobbing in her kitchen, unable to finish the call. I read on to find out that she, too, had lost twins at around twenty-three weeks. A boy and a girl. I couldn't believe it. How was this possible? I was entranced.

I spent the entire afternoon and evening reading her blog. When Brian went to sleep, I grabbed my laptop and brought it downstairs. Cuddled up with a blanket and a cup of tea, I read into the early hours of the morning, not stopping until I had read every single entry on her entire site. This woman was further into her grief journey than I was, but her story was *so* similar to mine. Her words consumed me, and I wanted so badly to reach out to her. I needed an account with the online blog company in order to comment, which, of course, I didn't have, so I searched and located an email address. I opened up my email and wrote:

Dear Audrey,

I found your blog tonight and I can't stop reading it. I just lost twins at almost 24 weeks, and I am really struggling. I just wanted to say thank you for putting this out there for me to find, and read, and relate. I didn't know anyone else felt the way I do. Do you have any other advice on how to survive this grief?

Sincerely,
Christy

The next morning, my heart started pounding when I saw her reply in my inbox. I opened it, breathless.

Dear Christy,

I'm glad you found my blog. It's been a year since I lost Z and L and I am still struggling, honestly. It helps me to write, and it might help you, too. It's a way to get it out. What are your babies' names? I'm so sorry this happened to you. Totally, totally sucks.

Xo,
A

It may not seem like much, but I was reduced to tears immediately. She had asked me my babies' names. She told me she was sorry, and that she knew it sucked. I almost couldn't believe it.

I was hooked. Through that first blog, I found a hundred more. I registered for an account and started leaving comments on the blogs I read, thanking them or asking questions. All day long, when I wasn't sleeping, I was reading blog posts. The stories were gut-wrenching. I read the story of a woman who was past her due date and went to the hospital worried about her baby, and they sent her home, only to have her return a few days later to find out that her baby was dead. I read the story of two women who had struggled to get pregnant only to be blessed with triplets, and for each and every one of those babies to die.

The stories were tragic, but there was a community out there. One of the triplet-loss moms, Rachel, had decided to raise monarch butterflies, and you could send her a request. When the butterflies were ready to be released, she would release them in honor of your baby. Another friend made angel wings with your baby's name on them and would mail them to you. Women would collect donations for hospital NICUs and bring tiny little baby outfits and blankets for bereaved parents to have. A woman in Australia offered to write your baby's name in the sand at the most beautiful beach, and she would send you a copy of the photo. There was even a blog where if you signed up and told them how much your baby weighed, they would send you a teddy bear that would weigh that exact amount for you to hold.

It was here, in this community of bloggers, that I slowly found my way again. I started my own blog and began writing on it every single day, sometimes twice or three times on an especially bad day. When I would log in and see that I had comments, my heart would soar, and I would read the ones that I received over and over again. "Oh, I have had that exact same thought!" would help ease the nagging in my heart that I was going insane. "Oh, man, that must have been rough. Hugs!" would be the validation that I needed that I wasn't overreacting and what I had gone through really *was* rough.

There were nights that I sat alone in our office, typing on a screen that I couldn't even see because tears were running down my face so much. It was as if writing it was finally letting it go. Not everything, and not always permanently, of course, but it made me feel so much lighter. And it showed. My husband noticed first. Something would set me off, and I'd think, "Wait until I blog about this—the girls won't *believe* what that stupid lady said to me!" This was such an improvement to the nasty, dark thoughts that were prevalent in my mind in those days. On rough days, Brian would ask, "Do you need some time to go and write?"

Many of my in-real-life friends had reached out to me in the beginning but had later stepped back. Looking back now, I don't really blame them—I guess I wouldn't have known what to do either. It's undeniably difficult to grasp the thought of me delivering two babies that died.

Loneliness and isolation, they sneak their way in. At first it doesn't feel so bad—being alone in your grief is "normal," right? It's normal not to answer your phone—you're *grieving*, after all. My very closest friends had come and cried with me and held my hand, but what is left to do after that? Slowly, I formed a routine. I'd answer an email, "Yes, I'd love to get together!" Intentionally vague, I'd put off actually setting a date or a place as long as I could.

As an actual date and time approached, I would start giving myself a pep-talk. "You've got this, Christy. It is ridiculous that you cannot go out to dinner with your *friends*. The ones who you love. Get it together, yo." Then the feelings that were creeping in would get so overwhelming that the only thing I could do was start thinking about how to get out of it. My excuses became more and more creative. I was "sick" a lot. My mother-in-law "needed" us quite often.

You do this enough times, and those invitations stop coming in. The couple-friends that we had spent so many Saturday nights with laughing, eating, and playing board games stopped calling, along with almost everyone else. I was a drag to be around, and I knew it. I could cry over just about anything, I was still having episodes of post traumatic stress, and no one could talk about babies or pregnancy or kids around me.

I could feel the "old me" continuing to slip away. That girl that laughed all the time and saw the best in everyone and always had fun was gone, nowhere to be found. She had been replaced, without a choice, without a chance to go back. Even *I* felt uncomfortable with the person I had become. I had to learn to love myself again, and until I could do that, I wanted to be alone.

Then came anger and selfishness. Today, when anyone comes to me for advice about how to comfort their friend who has just lost a baby, the first thing I tell them is, "Expect them to seem selfish and love them anyway. Their world has just stopped moving, and they cannot understand how yours can still go on." Sophie and Aiden were the only things on my mind, and it just was unfathomable to me that it wasn't like this for everyone else.

I couldn't believe people wouldn't stop and think before they said something in front of me. "Guess what! I'm having another grandbaby!" felt like a personal attack on me—didn't they know that would make me die on the inside?

I was no stranger to anger and disappointment. I grew up with a father whose temper was absolutely hellacious. For that very reason, I vowed never to be mad. And it had worked, up until Sophie and Aiden died. I started having bouts of rage, and I would just scream at nothing. I never let anyone see, not even my husband, really. But my anxiety would skyrocket because of something, even something insignificant, and then I would see red, pounding my fists on walls or screaming profanities, while I cried of embarrassment. This exacerbated my longing to just be alone, not letting anyone see how hard this really was. I wondered how my husband could still love me after seeing this. Seeing me. I wondered if I should ever even try to have another baby if I had all this anger.

Eventually, my online friends became more to me than just validation—they became my lifeline, and with few exceptions, my only social interaction. They were where I felt the safest, where I knew that no matter what I said, they would recognize my feelings and share in them. They knew that what I was feeling was normal, and they certainly didn't need me to try to convince them that I was okay. I was not okay—none of us really were—but we were together, the same, equals. These ladies of mine, they knew exactly what to say because they were living and breathing my life. They wouldn't ask me dumb questions, and they would call my babies by name, and they knew even the littlest things about me—like that each month on the thirteenth, we would get ice cream to celebrate Aiden and Sophie's birth. These other women told me they knew my twins would have been something great, and that they were so lucky to have me for a mom.

I was part of an actual, real community. We did our best to lift each other up out of this dark pit that was our lives, and we did it the only way we knew how—with the kind of empathy and support that only someone who has lived through your hell can give you.

One day I was sitting in my office, and I got an email comment telling me I had been nominated for something. "This must be fake," I thought. I clicked on the link, and I had been nominated by a fellow blogger for something called the "Honest Scrap Award." There was a little write up about my blog.

WOW! I'm telling you that I felt like I had won an Academy Award that day—I'm not even exaggerating! I was so totally proud of myself, and I probably really did cry. I started yelling, "Baby! Babe! Get in here! Guess what!?"

Brian came running in, "What? What is it? Are you okay?"

"I got an award! A blog award!"

I remember the look on his face, the hesitation when he tried to decipher whether or not I was being serious. But my grin must have convinced him. "That's so great," he said. "Show me!"

***

Then there was Bree. I haven't been able to actually find the very first comment that Bree left on my blog, but I remember it like it was yesterday because of something she said at the end. It was something like, "Hi! My name is Bree and I lost a baby too at 24 weeks, her name was Ella. Sophie and Aiden are so beautiful. Xoxo"

I had labored over the decision to put the twins' pictures on my blog. In 2009, I wasn't really on social media all that much, and putting pictures online still felt a little strange to me. Not to mention that most of the pictures I have of Sophie and Aiden are pictures of them after they died. Today, social media is a huge part of my life, and I post several pictures a week of my family, yet I have only ever posted one photograph of them, on a Facebook memorial site dedicated to them. It's a private site and only has a fraction of my friends on it. I am simultaneously desperate to show them off to the world and panicked about what people would think or say about them.

My babies were extremely premature. They were perfectly formed and looked like babies, though not the chubby cherub-like ones you are used to seeing. They weighed almost two pounds, were long and lithe and could stretch out their legs nice and far. They were also bright red and had bruises, and they both had what seemed like a million wires attached to their tiny noses and mouths. The pictures aren't easy to look at, even the touched-up ones. I find them to be beautiful, of course, but if I'm honest (my goal here), even *I* struggle to look at them sometimes. The photos haunt me. They are what could have been. Photographic evidence of my failure.

I dream of people asking to see their beautiful faces, see their features, notice that they have my nose or Brian's forehead. What stops me? I've seen the gut-wrenching comments on other posts. "Ugh, that is so disgusting/so morbid/who puts a dead baby on Facebook/it makes me uncomfortable/nobody wants to see that/keep it to yourself/ that is so gross/what the fuck is that?" There is a fear that my friends and family, the people I choose to surround myself with and love and protect, won't be able to look past the redness and blood and bruises to see that there is a child in the photo. My child. Fear that I will have to live with knowing who is capable of that and who is not. And if not, can I really blame them? What would I have thought if this hadn't become my story?

Bree's comment caught my attention because she had called my babies by name *and* told me they were beautiful, which was the equivalent of being enveloped in a warm hug. I clicked on her name and was taken to her blog, titled "My Baby Butterfly Ella." There, I saw that she had a list where you could sign up, and she would send you a butterfly cutout with your baby's name. I typed up an email with Sophie and Aiden's information and sent it off.

Soon we were emailing back and forth two or three times a day. Our stories were so similar. Her daughter had been born at the exact same gestation in March of 2009, which was only a month before the twins! She had Polycystic Ovarian Syndrome (PCOS) like me, and she was a teacher, too! She had lost her father to lung cancer only months before my father-in-law died of the same thing. She was estranged from her mother like I was from my father. (Wait, she sued you? Shut up! My dad sued us, too!) We had similar family hang-ups and both wished we could move far away. We both loved trashy reality TV, the only thing we could actually bear to watch and know it would be relatively safe from the issues we wanted to avoid. Frankly, it's pretty astounding when you add it all up.

We loved talking about our differences as well. Wisconsin and California may share the dairy industry, but that's about it. We would joke about how different her giant city is from my tiny little Midwestern town. (No, I'm serious, the only time we have a traffic jam is when you're stuck behind a tractor! Not even lying!) She is seriously "crunchy," like she makes her own sour cream out of cashews kind of crunchy. I eat fast food and drink (gasp!) diet soda. I am an avid reader, always wanting to talk about my current book. Of course, over the years, I've become a lot more health-conscious, thanks to her, and she'll read a new book if I can't stop talking about it.

While Brian was at work, I would write on my blog, comment on others, find new ones to read start to finish, and email Bree. I quickly found I could ask her anything (Do you already wish you were pregnant again?) and tell her anything (Like when I lied to a random lady at Target and told her I was pregnant with twins). I couldn't believe that I had a new best friend . . . and that I had found her on the internet!

My spirit was lifting, and my days were getting a little brighter. There is nothing like finding out that you are not alone.

CHAPTER 9 - A VERY, VERY DARK PLACE

From: StacyK@email.com
Subject: Are you OK?
To: Christywopat@email.com
Date: Thursday, June 18, 2009, 9:32 p.m.

Christy-

Hey. I have been reading your blog. I am glad you have this space to write out your feelings. I am very worried about you, though. Your thoughts seem so dark to me, and I am just not sure if you are OK or not. Of course I know that this is such a hard thing to go through, but are you really OK? I know I probably should not say this, but I am a little worried that you are in a depression or that you are depressed.

Do you have someone professional to talk to? Do I need to do something?

I just want you to know that I am here for you if you need me.

Stacy

From: Christywopat@email.com
Subject: Re:Are you ok?
To: StacyK@email.com
Date: Thursday, June 18, 2009, 11:47 p.m.

Hi Stacy,
So good to hear from you! I guess, well, I think I understand why you wrote. I know my blog posts are very sad, but to be honest, some of my thoughts are even worse. I want you to know that I'm OK. I'm not, like, suicidal or anything. I'm just really sad. Grief just kinda . . . sucks. But really, thank you for checking on me!

Love,
Christy

From: StacyK@email.com
Subject: Christy
To: Brianwopat@email.com
Date: Thursday, June 18, 2009, 9:43 p.m.

Brian,
Hi, this is Stacy, Christy's friend. I just was reading her blog. Are you reading it? I'm really worried about her. Do you really think she's OK? Let me know if you think there's something I should do. I'm worried.

Stacy

Brian came into the office where I was aimlessly scrolling through Facebook and reading blog posts. He carefully set down an envelope next to me. It was a big, fat envelope, and without even looking at the return address, I knew what it was.

"Are you looking forward to going back?" he asked, cautiously.

"Uh, no. I never want to go back. Ever," I added at the end, for emphasis.

"Well, you know the students miss you. And your coworkers. And this is what you're made for, you know. Once you get back, you'll be happy." He looked at me and gave me one of his fake smiles in a kind-of-cute attempt to help.

"Um . . . yeah, probably not. Everyone there is pregnant or has a baby, and I don't have mine, and I hate every stupid person in the whole freaking school. And I mean that." I minimized the screen on my computer and ran into my bedroom and flopped myself on my bed.

The truth is, I was really lucky because most loss mamas I know had to go back to work very quickly after their loss. Either their doctors would not excuse them, or they couldn't afford to take the time away from work, or they just felt pressure to return. Not to mention that a miscarriage is hardly considered something you should miss work for. I had the summer off in addition to my "maternity" leave because I am a school teacher. I continued to work on curriculum writing and other projects from my own house, but I had successfully avoided any kind of meeting that I actually had to attend in person for months.

I will say, also, that this long of a break helped but also hindered me. For me, the longer I avoid something, the harder it becomes to face—hello, anxiety! I had spent all summer worrying about all of the different things that could happen once I got back. Who would say something stupid? What would the kids say? What if everyone just pretended that nothing had happened?

I hadn't even been in my classroom, mostly for fear of running into people, and that was difficult for me. I was the kind of teacher who spent pretty long hours at school and a lot of weekends, especially in those early years of teaching. On top of that, when everything went to hell, I basically ended up in the emergency room on a Sunday night and was gone the rest of the year—with a sub who was not a trained French teacher. She spoke some French and really tried her best, but teaching a foreign language to sixth, seventh, and eighth graders is not the easiest thing ever, especially when you have to step into the fire and basically get burned. She never once even emailed me throughout my entire leave even though she must have had hundreds of questions.

In August, when I got that back-to-school packet, I was actually ready—I loved my students and my job—but the thought of seeing my coworkers made my stomach turn sour. There were several other teachers on staff who had been pregnant at the same time as me, and so they would have their babies, and I would not. Also, I knew there were people there who felt that I should have come back right away. I could just hear them talking to each other about how I needed to "move on." One male teacher on staff told a friend of mine that he "wished he could be on bedrest" like me. It infuriated me. *You want to lie in bed for weeks, dripping amniotic fluid every time you coughed or sneezed or moved, the very fluid that your baby needs to develop her lungs? Yeah, sounds like a great time, right? Asshole.*

I also had had enough experiences with people at this point to know that my colleagues would probably act really strange around me or possibly just ignore me. As time went on, I had started sorting people into different reaction camps:

The "I can't stand to be uncomfortable" camp: They feel really bad for you, but bringing it up would make *them* feel nervous or sad or awkward, so they are not saying a word.

The "You are making too big of a deal out of this" camp: They don't think you really have anything to be sad about, so they are also not saying a word.

The "Full head-tilt" camp: These are the people that start tilting their head and opening their arms for a hug the minute they see you. "How *are* you?" they croon.

The "It happened for a reason" camp: Full of clichés, this group is armed with seventeen different phrases ready to make you feel all better. None of them work.

The "This sucks, yo" camp: My favorite, obviously. They're your people. "Hey, so glad you are back. What happened to you sucks big time! I'm here if you need someone's kneecaps busted."

As the day approached, I wondered why the hell I didn't just go back to work shortly after they died? *What was I thinking?* I did this a lot—going back and forth between knowing I should take the time to grieve and heal and then feeling like I was being super dramatic. I mean, they weren't even alive for more than a day; what was my problem? There were times when I decided that I was just going to get over it. I was going to stop bringing them up, stop thinking about it, stop worrying about everyone else remembering them, and just freaking move on.

That, obviously, did not work. There was so much doubt about what I *should* be doing or how I *should* be acting. I felt horrible when I didn't say anything, but when I spoke up, people consistently made me feel as though I should really just shut up about it. They did this through words, gestures, body language, all the way down to the absence of interaction with my social media posts. A post of "Going to sell the baby furniture" would get three comments, from friends I hadn't seen since high school, while "Ewww, chunky peanut butter is gross" would get forty-two likes. I actually remember throwing a book when I saw that someone who posted that their dog had died got practically a million comments of people's heartfelt sympathy and my dead babies garnered next to none.

I am, admittedly, a very sensitive person. I sometimes over-analyze things, and I get my feelings hurt easily. However, reading people is a strength of mine, and I'm pretty intuitive. I definitely got the sense when my friends thought I was hurting "too much."

When I first started writing my blog, I had initially decided to share it with my friends and family so they could understand me better and keep up with my life. I also hoped that eventually it would be a family blog when I had living children some day.

Remember that lady who emailed to tell me that she was worried about whether or not she should "do something" about me? I had no idea what she was talking about. Did I want to get together? Is that what she was asking? Then she told Brian that I might need an intervention because I seemed like I was in *too much pain?* What could I do with that besides cry with frustration, and then laugh, and finally make my blog private so that only certain people had access to it? Not much. That night, however, I did go back in and read some of my blog entries. My pain was spilling off of the pages, and my words were very dark. I didn't need an intervention, I wanted to say. I needed my babies back alive. In retrospect, I'm sure she was just really worried that I was suicidal. Honestly, in the first few months, maybe even a year, I frequently wished I was dead so I could be with them. I also wished that I had died instead of them.

Although I sometimes had those thoughts, the feelings were fleeting; they passed quite quickly. What's more is that I never really stopped to linger on those thoughts, and I had no plans to do anything extreme. Many of my blogger mama friends would talk about having those same feelings—grief really plummets you into an abyss of very serious, very intense thoughts. I can see how reading those confessions would be alarming to people who are not living it. From the outside looking in and all that.

Suicide is nothing to mess around with. In a way, I am glad my friend reached out because it really made me reflect. It made me take a step back and observe what was happening. Postpartum depression is real and can be life-changing, and although I'm not really sure if I did have that in addition to my grief or not, it is something to discuss with your doctor.

Right when I started writing this book, I was out with some of my girlfriends for dinner, and I started telling them the story about this email as an example of what I might write about. Instead of the "Oh, people are so annoying" reaction I expected, there were a lot of hunched up shoulders and eye raises. "Well, you really *were* in a very, very dark place, Christy," one of my friends reminded me. "It's not like we were wrong." I guess everyone really thought I was ready to jump off a bridge. Who knew?

***

After all that happened, I couldn't help but to expect the worst as I prepared to go back. My first day back at school included a meeting for some of the teacher leaders in the school. The morning of the meeting, I woke up with a headache and a stomachache. I tried to eat breakfast and subsequently vomited. I wondered, *What would really happen if I didn't go?* I paced back and forth in my living room, coming up with endless excuses as to why I just *couldn't go.* Brian looked me in the eye and said, "Babe. It's time. What could really be so bad?"

As soon as I walked in, I could barely breathe and my cement shoes bound me to the floor, unable to move. The first teacher I saw greeted me with, "Christy! It's so good to see you! We've really, really missed you around here!" and her smile seemed genuine. I began to relax almost immediately—what had I been worried about? I had worked with these people for years! They knew me! It was all going to be all right!

As we sat down, the principal started with, "Good morning! Good morning, everyone! I'm so glad to see you all here! I hope you had a great summer. We have a lot to do today, but we're going to begin with an ice breaker!" I groaned on the inside. Seriously, gag me! Do all workplaces do this, or is it just a school thing?

"Let's go around the table and each share two things that were great about our summer!" She grinned and looked around the table, trying to make eye contact with everyone.

Immediately, my heart started pounding and my hands started sweating. I wracked my brain. What was good about my summer?

What was good? Was there anything good? THERE WAS NOTHING GOOD ABOUT MY SUMMER BECAUSE MY BABIES DIED. Oh, God, please don't call on me first. Shit. Damn it! No!

Someone across the table from me started. "Well, the best thing about my summer was that my little boy learned to roll over. It was honestly the most amazing thing. I set him down in his crib and walked away, and when I came back? He was on his belly! I couldn't believe it! It was AMAZING!"

My head began to swirl. I could feel the tears rise immediately to the brims of my eyelids. The burning feeling inside needed to be choked down, or I was seriously going to break.

The next person began, "Honestly, the best thing about my summer was just being able to watch my kids grow and have the time to be with them without working."

"This summer we took our first family vacation-slash-road trip to South Dakota! We got to see Mount Rushmore, which my kids adored, and my Emily got her driver's license, which was life changing, and Eric, he . . ."

Tears were stinging my eyes. I knew everyone could tell. When it got to me, I could barely manage words. I said, "To be honest, there wasn't a lot about my summer that was great. I'm sorry. I wish I could say that there was. But we did take a trip to Las Vegas, I guess."

My voice was breaking, and tears were streaming down my face. Every single person at that table gave me the sideways head tilt. A few looked away. I felt so stupid, like such a spectacle. I couldn't look up. I prayed they would move on.

The rest of the morning passed without incident although the redness never did leave my cheeks. I was so embarrassed for showing my emotions so freely like that and for not doing a better job of faking it. I did start feeling a little better after a talk with a colleague. She told me that everyone had been worrying about me and asked about how I was doing. They were really, really glad I was back. I tried to believe her.

I was on my way to the lunchroom when I heard a few ladies give a squeal. "Oh my goodness!!!! He is *so* perfect!"

I turned and saw a woman pushing a stroller with one hand, holding onto a tiny, newborn baby boy in the crook of her other arm. This particular coworker was due just a few days after I was, and so our team at work had scheduled a baby shower for both of us at once. My water broke the week before the date of the shower. She had the baby shower and a baby. I had—nothing. I couldn't look. I couldn't think. I couldn't move.

Tears were rushing down my face like a tidal wave, and the room started to swirl. I knew I couldn't be there anymore. I ran out and didn't stop running until I got to the office. I went into one of the secretary's offices down the hall and closed the door. She wasn't in there, thankfully, and so I sat down and let the sobs wrack my entire body. I was just so defeated. So tired and so defeated.

I didn't go back, and no one ever did ask me where I went.

***

At the time the twins died, I was a middle school teacher (I teach elementary school now), and I taught a subject that allowed me to teach every single student in the middle school—around 800 students. The day Sophie and Aiden died, the principal called all of the students into a classroom and had the teachers read them a statement about what had happened to me.

"Mrs. Wopat delivered her twins yesterday. Today, we found out that they were too small and too sick, and they passed away in the hospital. Mrs. Wopat is okay and will update us when she can."

Theoretically, every person in my school got this message. But I would run into teachers in town or at meetings, and they would seem confused about where my twins were. Around two years after my loss, I was blessed to deliver a beautiful baby girl. I'll explain more about this wonderful gift soon, but for now, just know that Avery was my only living child. I was at a district meeting when a woman approached me and said, "How are your kids?"

I remember just sucking in my breath and trying to center myself. "Avery is good! She's walking and talking already!"

Confused look. (Please just move on, please just talk to someone else, please just don't.)

"Right, but how are the twins? They must be, what, two or three already?"

At this point, I literally just turned and walked away. I pretended like I heard my name and awkwardly just left. I wasn't much in the mood for correcting people then, and maybe not even now.

There is, however, one coworker from our school district who is somehow still confused seven years later! Everytime my husband or I saw him over the years, I noticed that he would look around, or he'd mutter something under his breath, asking if we had all the kids, or where were the rest of them, or something like that. I never really corrected him, because it just didn't seem worth it—worth the pain for me, I mean.

One day, we saw him out at a community fundraising event that involved bicycle races for the children. The races were grouped so that the kids were racing against other kids of the same age. My daughter, who was four at the time, was warming up with the other racers, while my son, who was eighteen months old, was sitting in the stroller with us, waiting. This colleague came up to us and said hello, and then spent some time looking back and forth from my daughter to my son. He nodded at my son, and asked, "Why isn't he racing?"

"Well," I replied, "He's not old enough."

"How can she be old enough, but not him? You have . . . Well . . . Wait. Where are the twins?"

Then he started looking all around me as if I had some extra kids hiding somewhere. I looked at Brian, urging him to take this one.

"You have twins, right?" He continued looking around frantically until I answered.

"We had twins. They died. Do you remember? They died." I looked again at Brian, who looked at the ground.

"Oh, shit. Oh, damn it. That's right. I think I . . . did I know that? You know, I, uh, you heard I got a divorce, right? Yeah, last year I got a divorce. It's been really hard. So, I get it. I know what it's like."

I could only just stare at him. He started walking slowly backward, away. "Well, I gotta, uh, go. My daughter, she's, uh, she's ready to start her race. Bye, you guys."

To this day, every time I see him, I have a good laugh on the inside. Not at him, of course, just at the whole situation. Well, maybe a little bit at him. Thank goodness for laughter! Often it's the only way I get through this life. I just cannot believe that I still have to stumble through all of this, so many years later!

Sometimes people just come right out and ask me, "How are the twins?" That's actually a really tough one because I just want to bluntly answer, "Still dead." But most people will not think that's funny at all, so I don't. The problem is, I really don't know what to give for an answer besides the truth. Frankly, sometimes I just say, "Fine, thanks," because I really don't know my way out of it. I just don't know how else to answer without being so brutally honest, which isn't always what people want.

Whenever I would try to vent my frustrations about people and what they'd say to me, I would hear:

"You know, Christy, you shouldn't judge people for their reactions to you. They don't know how to act."

"You just have to be the better person."

"You need to take the high road."

"People just don't know what to say. You have to forgive them."

"People just don't understand."

I tried. I did. I tried to be understanding. I tried not to judge. I tried to be the bigger, better person. And sometimes I was successful. I promise! But other times, words would cut me to the core, so far deep that the high road was an impossibility for me. I wanted to be strong, and I wanted to be brave, but . . . the pain made me fragile. It was all I could do to get up and face the day, let alone help everyone else be okay with their insensitive words.

There were very few words that comforted me. When I went back to work, "We missed you," and "I am so sorry for this horrible thing that happened to you," were just about the only things I wanted to hear. When someone you know is grieving, whether or not you think they are grieving too hard, or for too long, or for no reason—none of those things matter. It doesn't matter what *you* think about *their* grief! Support them and tell them you are so sorry that this is happening to them.

I know that sometimes it becomes difficult to listen to and support a grieving friend. Sometimes they tell you the same story again and again. Sometimes it feels like they're whining. At times, you might want to yell, "OMG I get it! *Enough* already!" It's not fun to be around someone who tears up at what seems like something so trivial. You may even start to dread being with them.

Your grieving friend might not show up. One of my friends was pregnant at the same time I was. Shortly after I lost the twins, I got a baby shower invitation in the mail. I was *furious*! I sobbed. I threw something. I called Brian at work and raged and whined. I typed out emails that I didn't send.

"The *audacity* of her!" I cried to my mom. "How could she send me a baby shower invitation *now*?!"

"Well, honey, she doesn't know. I'm sure she wasn't trying to hurt you. She's your friend!"

"Well, if she were *really* my friend, she would have known that this would kill me. That her ignoring the fact that I have TWO DEAD BABIES would make me want to DIE."

"Okay, well, honey, I have to go. Someone is coming into the office."

I waited for someone to stick up for me. I waited for the phone call that would say, "Hey, just checking on you to see if you're all right. I know going to a baby shower would be impossible for you right now."

That never happened, and it was a bitter pill to swallow. What I've learned from this, after many years of heartache, is that whatever I needed, whatever I was feeling, I had to say it. What seemed like common sense to me—my babies just died; therefore, I could not possibly go to a baby shower—was not common sense to everyone. And people aren't sure how to navigate this loss with you. My friend didn't want to leave me out. She probably really wanted to see me. And she would never have sent that invitation had she known how much despair it would cause me.

Your grieving friend might seem selfish. I realize, too, that it's also probable that this friend of mine thought that I was absolutely acting this way. She may have called her mom and said, "How can she not come to this baby shower, this thing that is so important to me? How unfair is that?"

Here is where I wish I could tell you that we are still great friends. That I called her and we worked it out. But instead, I have to tell you that to this day I haven't seen her or communicated with her short of unfriending her on Facebook, then friending her again years later. I've never told her why I did that or even acknowledged that it happened. And . . . I still harbor hurt feelings. I know! It's totally not fair! And it's not even really her. I love her. I'm not angry with her. But it stuck with me, and I was never brave enough to bring it up to her.

And now that I am probably brave enough to tell her, it feels ridiculous bringing it up this late in the game. Does she even remember? Would she even care? Would I insult her by telling her how much she hurt me? I think it's too late now, but I really wish I could have been more honest then. The outcome would be different, surely.

In this situation, I wasn't really being selfish. I was doing the only thing I could do to emotionally survive at the time. It was protection. But there were certainly other selfish times! Frankly, nobody else's problems really mattered to me during those first few months. *Everything* seemed trivial to me. You lost your job? MY BABIES DIED. You're sad your child is going away to college? Oh, well, MY BABIES DIED. Knowing that this was awful, I tried to stop it. The inner dialogue went something like this:

She couldn't find the boots she really, really, really wanted in her size. So she is very upset. They couldn't even order any for her. And those were the ONLY boots that fit her. Like, REALLY fit her. So she is mad. So, what can you say back? Think. Think. This is ridiculous. Who cares about effing boots? UGH. At least she doesn't have dead babies. People are so annoying. Okay, she's waiting. Whadda we got?

And then I would spit out something vaguely acceptable, and friend probably (hopefully) didn't notice.

Because of this, I have to admit that sometimes I'm just not as good of a friend as I was before. I still look at my life as two distinct parts: before the twins and after the twins. Before, I had always been the supportive friend. The one you could call whenever you needed anything. I was understanding and always ready to give advice. You could count on me! After the twins, it got much harder not to judge people because whatever they were going through "wasn't bad enough."

To some extent, I still hope that my friends would consider me supportive. But, I'm more absent.

My memory, my attention span, my ability to concentrate, and my temper all got worse after the twins, too. Time and a lot of work have slowly helped to improve my memory and attention span, and it took anti-anxiety medication to help my temper. Grief has permanently changed me, for better and for worse. It's like they say. Your whole life really can change in an instant. I heard that pop, felt my water break, and now I am forever going to be the "after."

CHAPTER 10 - I CAN'T LOOK

From: Christy Wopat christywopat@email.com
Subject: To Bree from Christy
To: Bree@email.com
Date: Sunday, November 8, 2009, 11:18 a.m.

Hi, Bree :) It's Christy from almostamother :)

I just wanted to write and check in with you and see how you were doing. I can't believe how scared I am of everything. I don't know how to even make it through the first u/s to see if there is a heartbeat. The first one we had of those the first time around I was too ignorant to even know I should be worried about it!

Now I'm worried about everything and so far my peri doesn't want to do anything differently with this pregnancy. Can I ask you what diagnosed you with IC? What did you decide about the cerclage?

Who have you told? I told my mom, looking for support because she lost a baby at full-term and has been through this. Then I saw her this weekend, and she had already bought a little outfit.

It made me want to scream! I don't know why, and I know it's irrational, but I feel like that is jinxing it or something. If she buys things, I don't even want to know about it. It's so weird.

Ugh. It's a big mixture of hope and fear but mostly I feel too afraid to be hopeful.

When is your due date? I still don't exactly know, but it'll be around the first week of July.

Ok, well, I just asked you about a million questions. Sorry about that!

Anyway, write back when you can/want to/need to!

xxoo
Christy :)

On Monday, November 9, 2009, 9:14 a.m., Bree <Bree@email.com> wrote:

Hi Christy,

I'm glad you emailed. It's good to hear from you. I feel ya on so many levels.

After finding out I was pregnant, I had two good beta tests. But, then was told I had to wait until 7 1/2 weeks for an ultrasound. I couldn't believe I had to wait that long. I actually got to see Ella at 5 1/2 because I had spotting. I guess I was spoiled. I freaked out and convinced myself that I had a blighted ovum or an ectopic pregnancy. About a week before my first scheduled ultrasound, I started having intense back pain only on one side. I made my husband take me to the ER where we waited for 5 hours for an ultrasound. Turns out, a kidney stone was causing the pain and the baby was fine. Though, the second I left, I thought, Okay the baby was alive then and there, but is it alive now? It's crazy I haven't had an early miscarriage (unless the chemical pregnancy counts), but that I'm so afraid of one. I didn't think I'd be nervous until I got closer to when I lost Ella. Anyways, my point is . . . If you don't think you can wait til 11/20, you could always go to the ER and complain of back pain. :)

I haven't even seen a peri yet. I get to see him in two weeks to talk about my cerclage. After I lost Ella, my doctor pretty much concluded that I lost Ella because of IC (incompetent cervix). She said that something like 80 percent of 2nd trimester losses are due to IC. And, the fact that my cervix dilated without any cramping or contractions is true IC. I went to Labor and Delivery because I had lost my mucus plug. That was my only sign of labor. I've had my doubts though that IC was the cause of my loss. I haven't had any damage done to my cervix (that I know of). My doctor said that it is congenital—something I was born with. My sister has fertility issues and has adopted all of her babies, so I wonder if she did get pregnant if she'd have IC too.

Since you are most likely pregnant with a singleton this time, you may be fine. The weight and pressure difference may make a huge difference. But, if I were you, if it were going to make you feel better, I'd insist on a cerclage. Are you going to get progesterone shots starting at 16 weeks? They have been shown to prevent preterm labor. I'm going to do them even though my doctor says I shouldn't need them if the cause was IC. But, she's willing to do anything that may help.

I've pretty much decided to have the TVC. I'd love to have the transabdominal cerclage, but I just feel like it's too late. There's no way the insurance is going to approve it, and if they were they wouldn't approve it in the next few weeks. My doctor swears that a TVC is the way to go. She said she's never had a patient lose a baby after getting a TVC early on. And, she's been practicing for 18 years. So, I'm excited to talk to the perinatologist in a few weeks since he is the one who will be doing the procedure.

I don't have many friends anymore. I've kind of isolated myself since losing Ella. But, the people who are still around know I'm pregnant. First of all, they knew we were trying to conceive and when they asked I just couldn't lie to them. Plus, what's the use of not telling anyone until you're out of the first trimester? I did that with Ella and I still lost her. I figure I could have waited until I started to show, but I'm already popping out and wearing my maternity jeans. And, I also figure if I lose another one, I'm going to want people to know. I haven't told my employers and we haven't told my in-laws. We will probably tell them at Thanksgiving—I'll be 12 weeks then, anyway. I don't mind if people know I'm pregnant, but I want them to understand two things— 1. I'm still very much grieving for Ella and 2. It is possible that we may lose this baby, too.

My due date is 6/18. Exactly three weeks before Ella's due date 7/10 (which is probably around the time when you are due). I'm 8 weeks 2 days today. Praying and hoping we both make it to the summer.

I so badly want to cherish this pregnancy, every minute of it. But, it is so hard not to be nervous and protect yourself from the possibility of losing again.

Sorry I wrote so much. It just feels good to work through everything and try to process all this.

Talk soon!

Bree :)

On Monday, November 9, 2009, 2:24 p.m., Christy Wopat <christywopat@email.com> wrote:

Oh, BREE!!! So much of what you say I feel. I am TERRIFIED of an early loss. I don't have any morning sickness really yet, which 1) is normal, I'm only 5 weeks and 2) I had so much with the twins I'm not even sure I'd notice it, but I'm convinced that I'm not really pregnant. I took another test today. Can you say SPAZ?

I'm so sorry about all that pain and that kidney stone! How scary! So glad to hear the baby was fine, though.

So, I lost my mucus plug, too. I didn't know what it was. I called my doctor, and she said not to worry about it. If I could change anything in my entire life, I would have walked my butt right into labor and delivery right then. But I didn't, because the thought of that terrified me, and a week later my water broke.

My peri thinks it was an infection eating away at the sac. He thinks I didn't have IC because I had a long and painful labor once I finally started (2 weeks after my water broke). There's no way to know which came first. Chicken or the Egg. I asked about 17p shots and he said the research doesn't *really* support them. I want them anyway, and plan to ask again. There are no known negative side effects, so why the heck not??? I don't care what they cost. I'm just so scared. I just wish I knew. I just wish so much.

Every two minutes I feel like bursting into tears. Then I picture it summer, and I have a baby with me, and I feel this hope. It's a perfect storm of hope & fear.

I had to tell my boss today because I have all these appointments coming up already, and I need to get people to cover for me. She was really nice, and I just hope that she doesn't tell anyone. She really doesn't have the right. I went today to get the H1N1 shot since I work in a school. That freaks me out! Even though I've already "had it" I got the vaccine anyway. Vaccines scare me :(but all the stuff about pregnant ladies and babies dying scares me more!

Ok, maybe we can work together somehow to cherish the moments of this pregnancy even if we are scared. What could we do? Write each other with one special thing every now and then?

> Also . . . you're not going to believe this . . . my due date is 7/10. Exactly the same date as Ella. Can you believe it?
>
> Well, I have to go. Write me ANY time as MUCH as you want!!!!!! !!!!!!!!!!!!!!!!!!!!!
>
> P.S. Your last name is so cool! How do you say it?

"Okay, Christine," the doctor said, sitting down heavily on his stool, causing it to roll backward into the table. "What is it that I can do for you today?"

"Well, we just wanted to talk. I mean . . . I guess we just wanted to ask about our next pregnancy, if, well, if there is going to be one." I shifted in my seat. Did he even remember who I was? My mind flashed to him standing over me, repeating that "You can never trust a second twin!" as he haphazardly held my ankle up in the air, staring at an ultrasound machine, while I pushed.

"So, right then. What is it that you wanted to know?"

I looked helplessly over at Brian. He looked at the floor, deferring this to me. What the hell? I didn't even know what to say. Wasn't the doctor supposed to do most of the talking?

"Well," I started. "We want to know what we could do differently, I guess, to make sure . . . well, so that the same thing won't happen again." I could hear myself saying the words, but they came out shakier than I hoped.

He turned his chair back toward the table, this time his elbow making a big thud as he began to *click, click, click* his way around the screen.

"Okay, uh-huh," he mumbled. "Preterm, premature rupture of membranes, multiples, live birth, both deceased." His eyes scanned the page as Linda, his nurse, entered the room. Just the sight of her made my heartbeat quicken, anxiety rising. ("Honey, I think it's time we start thinking about funeral arrangements.") She sat down in a chair and pulled out a notepad and pen.

"Well. I think, really, we won't change a thing. I don't think you had preterm labor. I think we'll get you pregnant. If you have a single pregnancy, we'll measure your cervix to make sure it stays nice and long. And if you have twins again . . . well, we'll get you a valium." His laughter boomed throughout the small room. My eyes focused on a plastic model of a uterus with ovaries. I wondered if he ever actually used it.

My thoughts came rapid-fire: *You mean I want my cervix to be long? How can a cervix be long? I don't even really know what a cervix is. Was mine short with the twins? Is that all I need to worry about, is a cervix? A short one?*

I went for the big guns, "But, I want a cerclage! And 17p shots. And check-ups every week . . ." my voice trailed off.

His eyes could have rolled. Maybe they started to. He sighed. "You don't need a cerclage. You had a long-enough labor, and you took a long time to dilate. I think you were just unlucky. A multiple pregnancy is very different from a singleton one. *That* is what we will do differently. Go get pregnant, if you want, and we'll talk about it then."

I stood up and then sat back down. My temples thudded as the blood rushed up. "Doctor, I am terrified. I don't really know what happened with the twins. I don't know why it happened. If I was unlucky then, how do I know I won't be unlucky now?"

He stood up, grabbing my chart. "You don't," he finished and closed the door behind him.

As we walked out of the clinic, Brian grabbed my hand. "He seemed really optimistic! Like it was just a fluke, ya know? Hey, if we got pregnant on the first try, when would they get here?"

His words cut like ice.

"Babe, there is no 'they.' There won't ever be a 'they' again," I scolded. "One baby this time. There will be *only* one."

The first thing I did when I got home was to grab my computer. I stretched out in bed and Googled "17p shots." Bree had mentioned them to me, and several of my blogging friends had mentioned them, too. I was really quite determined to get them. So determined that I thought maybe I could order them online from Canada or Mexico and give them to myself. I opened up the hospital's website and typed a message to my doctor's nurse. "Hello, again, I just wanted to ask one more time about the 17p shots for premature labor. Once I get pregnant, I'd like to revisit this in time to start taking them at sixteen weeks. Thank you!"

Thoughts of being pregnant again had consumed me since even before Aiden and Sophie were dead. Maybe even before they were born. And when I say consumed, I'm not exaggerating. I dreamed of having a baby for so long, and I had come so close. It took over two years to get that positive pregnancy test, and then the ultimate betrayal. It was irrational in one sense, to be grieving so hard but just wanting to be pregnant, but on the other hand, it was obvious that I should feel this way. The perinatologist had told us to wait six months, but of course I kept taking pregnancy tests, convinced I had accidentally gotten pregnant. Of course we were barely having sex, and I was infertile, but you know, I had heard someone tell me about someone they knew that "used to be infertile, but after they were pregnant, they just kept popping babies out." Right.

As the pages of the calendar turned, however, that familiar mixture of excitement and dread arrived. My emotions were flip-flopping all over the place. One minute I couldn't wait to be pregnant. I would daydream about putting a new nursery back together and play out me walking into the teachers' lounge with a baby picture to show everyone. The next minute I would feel so sick, knowing I was insane to try this again. *What the hell are you doing?* I'd ask myself. *You're going to inflict all this pain on your family, again?*

Talking to friends brought more clichés. "If there is no risk, there is no reward," I'd get reminded. On the other hand, "If you don't risk anything, you risk everything." My mother stayed quiet. She wouldn't take a side. Didn't want to talk about it. Brian, my eternal optimist, didn't even see this as taking a risk. He just knew everything would be okay.

But then I remembered my people. My "internet friends." Our group of "baby loss moms" had all lost our babies within a month or two of each other, and now we were making decisions about what would happen next. Some women had quickly decided to be done—either families were complete or their loss had proven to be too much of a risk for a subsequent pregnancy. Others wanted to try again, but decided it wasn't worth the risk.

I went and blogged about it. I laid it all out on the page. My terror. My relentless longing for a baby to hold. I wrote about the doctor and the fact that no one could even really tell me what had happened to make me lose the twins. I hit submit and waited for comments.

I read other blogs and articles. Cried about it. Tried to talk with Brian about it. In the end, though, the decision was mine. It was my body, my mind that would have to do all the work. I had to be the one to give the final say.

Here again, I wish I had some sort of feeling or intuition leading my way. I was desperate for someone to just tell me what to do or give me some statistics that could help my decision-making process. I needed a pro and con list. In order to do that, I needed more information.

***

I sat on the edge of the chair, my leg bouncing relentlessly. I heard a faint knock on the door, and the perinatologist hurried in, his eyes on the file in his hands, not on me. "Ah, Christine. I see you're back. What can I do for you this time?"

Breathe in, breathe out. "Well, first I was wondering if you had gotten my request to take a look at the research about the progesterone shots?"

Without looking up, he picked up a pen and scribbled on a notepad. I cleared my throat. He turned to look at me, as if he had forgotten I was there. "Uh, yes, it's as I said before. You didn't have preterm labor. You don't need a cerclage or progesterone shots. There's no research that shows those shots even work. My position has not changed."

My mind flashed back to his infamous words, "Christine, you can't push until you've had a contraction. Never trust a second twin. I'll tell you what we'll change this time; we'll have one baby instead of two."

Breathe in, breathe out. Slowly, I began, "Doctor, I came here today, really, only to ask you one question." I looked him right in the eyes. "If . . . okay, if I were your daughter, would you tell me to try again? For another baby?"

Air escaped from between his lips like a deflating balloon. "Well," he began. "Well, I guess I would have to say that I would. I would tell my daughter to try again."

My heart exploded.

"Oh, and I would also tell *my daughter* she didn't need the progesterone shots," he finished. "Come back when you're pregnant."

***

As Brian and I got into bed and pulled up the covers, I began to feel so ridiculous. I was already red in the face and strangely nervous. We had only made love maybe twice since the babies died, and both times I had barely made it through. And to be frank, I didn't really want to now, either. My plan was to initiate it tonight so that he knew I was ready. But was I? I felt like a teenager all over again, not knowing how to make love to someone I had been married to for years.

The thing about intimacy is that it is so…intimate. My heart felt so dead inside, and on top of that I didn't care about myself at all. I had gained weight, my body had changed with pregnancy, I didn't change out of sweatpants, I wasn't eating healthy food or exercising. I was grieving, and I was depressed.

Brian hadn't reached over to touch me in months, either. I had been so grateful for the doctor imposed six-week post-birth intercourse ban, but as soon as it was over, Brian had tried. I mostly just pretended to be asleep, which was awful. We should have talked about it.

Had we talked about it, Brian would have said that he was terrified of hurting me, terrified of making another baby, terrified of making me grieve again. He couldn't think about it without thinking about the twins, which isn't exactly a huge turn-on. He would have told me he was exhausted from working and worrying about me and his own grief.

Had we talked about it, I would have explained that I loved him so much, but that I didn't love *me*, and that made me feel alone. Lonely, even. That I didn't feel like doing anything but crying and sleeping, and that feeling good made me feel bad. I felt like I didn't deserve to feel good.

But now, here we were, with the green light from the doctor to "go ahead and try." Online, there were a bunch of acronyms for it: DTD (do the deed), TBD (the baby dance), and TTC (trying to conceive). Lying in bed, like two strangers instead of two young, married people. In such a short time, such a distance had grown.

That night, and for many subsequent nights, I just "had sex." I have never had a one-night stand. I don't know what it's like to have sex with someone I don't know, or someone I'm not in love with. But I felt so awkward, so disconnected. I felt so fake. And the worst part was that the whole time all I could think about was that I didn't want to be trying to get pregnant *again*. I wanted to *still* be pregnant. I wanted my twins. I wanted Sophie and Aiden.

Years ago we tried for two years. In the beginning, it was fun. Then came the Googling: "Will different positions make it more likely to get pregnant?" or "How will I know if I ovulated?" Spending hundreds of dollars on ovulation tests and pregnancy tests, only for them to show up negative every single time. Tears of despair each time my period would eventually show up, never in a routine cycle, but just whenever it damn well pleased.

This time should be different, though. After all this time, I had proven that with a little help, my body could do it. Well, it could get pregnant. Staying pregnant I wasn't sure about. Every time we would finish, I would wonder, "Do I even want to be pregnant?" Honestly, I would flip back and forth emotionally so quickly and so often that I also added to my list of worries that I was not even going to be emotionally stable enough to raise a child, even if I could manage to have one.

There wasn't a night when I wasn't still haunted by the trauma that we had just experienced. Could I really put myself through that again? I felt crazy to even try, yet I couldn't *not* try, either. There was something there, a nagging, telling me that I needed to at least try.

***

As I sat on the edge of the toilet, watching the little hourglass blinking, turning, blinking, turning, I thought about something my sister had told me once. She had read in a book or seen somewhere on a show that there are people who believe in the fact that our souls are eternally linked to the souls of our loved ones. That even if someone you love dies, they come back into your life, somehow. It might be through a new friend you meet, or a niece or nephew, but somehow they manage to find you again.

Could it be that Sophie and Aiden's souls were meant to be mine? Would they come back to me, through a new baby? This was an uncomfortable idea to consider. Is that what I wanted? Their souls with me? Everyone told me their souls were with Jesus, although I had trouble finding out details about that. What would they look like in Heaven? When I got there, would I know how to find them?

When I was a very little girl, young enough that I could barely talk, I told my aunt that I "had a couch like that when I was old like Grandma." My aunt has traveled the world and at the time, I think, had settled on Buddhism, and she was sure I had been reincarnated. Off and on throughout my life, I have found my mind wandering back to this conversation and what it could have meant. Could souls have a second try? A second try at life when the first one wound up as terrible as it did for the twins?

"Babe? What's going on? Are you okay?" Brian stood in the doorway in his pajamas, rubbing his eyes. It was 4:00 in the morning, the middle of the night, and I had gotten up to use the bathroom. My heart started pounding when I looked at the clock and realized that it was "morning" enough for "first morning urine," otherwise known as the best urine to use when testing for pregnancy hormone levels. I went straight for a pregnancy test, deciding I wouldn't wake him unless I needed to.

It was late October, and we had done one round of fertility meds. They were new, different from the ones we had used with the twins. They would help me ovulate at the right time but had a much lower percentage chance of a multiple pregnancy. The fertility doctor was so kind, but how could anyone know that what I wanted more than anything was another set of twins, and we were going to do anything to make sure that wasn't going to happen again. Mid-cycle, I went in for an ultrasound to make sure I didn't have too many big follicles that would raise my chances for a multiple pregnancy. Luckily, it looked great.

"I can't look," I said. "It's going to be negative. We got pregnant on the first round of Clomid with the twins, so we're not going to get that lucky again. Plus, my body probably knows I'm too scared to be pregnant right now, anyway."

"What can't you look at?" he asked, confused. He walked into the bathroom and grabbed the test from the counter. "Oh, is it already time to test? Why didn't you wake me up?"

I glared at him. "Because I didn't want to make a big deal out of another fucking negative pregnancy test," I snapped. "Because I thought I'd see it was negative, and then I'd go back to bed, and I wouldn't have to bother you."

"Well, would you have woken me up once you saw it was positive?" he teased, ignoring my outburst. He handed me the test.

It said 'pregnant.' My mind and heart began fighting, and I was gasping for air. I looked to my husband for direction. He was grinning. I wanted to smile, too. I wanted to cry. Suddenly I wanted to take it back. All of it. I didn't want to be pregnant.

A movie started playing in my mind. It was me, standing at the funeral home. A man was handing me an urn. "I'm so sorry, again, ma'am," he was saying. *This time, I'll hold the baby longer. I'll look at him and maybe give him a bath. I'll make my family come and meet him, and I'll make sure he knows he's loved. I'll use that photography company. I'll have a service so my friends can come and say good-bye. I'll . . .*

"Um, hello? Why aren't you saying anything? Babe?" Brian pulled me to him.

"Come here and give me a hug! Why are you crying? WE ARE PREGNANT! We are going to have a baby! Everything is going to be just fine."

Just fine. Everything is going to be just fine.

CHAPTER 11 - BABY, STAY IN

I sat in the teachers' lounge at school, slowly stirring my yogurt. I felt headachy and tired, and I wished that somehow the seventh graders who were coming for me in ten short minutes would disappear so I could take a nap.

A science teacher walked in and sat down next to me. "How are you, Christy? Things good with you guys? Ready for Christmas break?"

"Fine. Good. Yes, so ready for break. How about you?" The words came out, almost on their own. I was programmed. Programmed to respond, to be polite. I almost laughed at myself, thinking how it would sound if I answered honestly.

I would say, "Well, I'm pregnant, or at least I think I am because I haven't actually had another ultrasound to make sure. I am up all night having nightmares about my water breaking, yet I don't even really have enough amniotic fluid yet to actually be able to break. In a week I have to face my first Christmas with two dead babies, and no one I know seems to actually care all that much. The only pregnancy symptom I have is fatigue, which could just be because I'm grieving . . . and I'm not even half as nauseous as I was with the twins, so I'm pretty sure this baby has died, too. In fact, I think it maybe even died this morning."

Instead, I forced a smile and packed up my yogurt and headed back to my room. I opened up my email and began one to Bree.

> Dear Bree,
> I can't take it anymore. I'm going to the ER after school. I need to hear a heartbeat. Please advise.

My email pinged right away.

> Do it. But call your doctor first and see if you can go there instead of ER.

I still had five minutes before the end of my lunch period, so I grabbed my purse. I had a business card for Linda, the perinatologist's nurse. I left a short message on her cell phone, pleading my case.

After school, I listened to my voicemail. "Hello, Christine. I got your message. We can squeeze you in for a quick heartbeat check; that's no problem. Just check in when you get here, and we'll sneak you in between patients."

While I waited for relief to set in, I suddenly realized that maybe this wasn't what I wanted. What would I do if there was no heartbeat? I wasn't ready to deal with that. What if they told me that whatever they thought they had seen at my five-week ultrasound never really turned out to be anything at all, and I'd have to go back to the fertility clinic and start over? I'd have to lie on the table listening to my own heartbeat and nothing else. I bet they'd search for a while. The nurse would say, "Oh, please don't worry, sometimes it takes a little bit to find it." My heart would sink, and I would know that it was over.

Shuddering, I started drafting a text to Brian. At the very least, I needed to have someone with me.

> Can u meet me at the clinic downtown after you leave work? I can wait for you in the waiting room.

As soon as we walked in the room, my heart started pounding so intensely that I had to stop for breath. I knew I was going to have a miscarriage. I wasn't sick enough. I wasn't hormonal enough. At least I would know so that I could deal with it.

The nurse tightened the blood pressure cuff around my arm, and she put her hand on mine. "Try to relax," she said. "We'll take good care of you."

I laughed. "I don't exactly think I can relax right now, but I will try." I began trying to take deep breaths.

"130 over 82," she reported, ripping the Velcro cuff off my arm. "Looks like your blood pressure knows you are nervous, too. We'll take it again after we've heard the heartbeat, okay? Let's get you up on the table, and you can lift your shirt up to your bra line."

Brian helped me up on the table. I watched her squirt the cold, blue gel on my abdomen. I tried to focus on my breathing, a technique I had learned from the grief counselor. "Okay," said the nurse. "You're going to feel the wand on your belly soon. Remember, sometimes it takes a minute to find the heartbeat, especially in the beginning like this."

My heart couldn't take it. She moved the wand around slowly, carefully, as the Doppler made its obnoxious crackling sound. She slowed down, the familiar swish, swish sound came, and I held my breath. It's a wonder I didn't pass out.

"Well, there's Mom's heartbeat," she said, not making eye contact with me. She moved down lower on my abdomen, slowing the wand, searching.

Tears sprang to my eyes. She couldn't find it. I knew it. *I knew it.* She'd be searching forever, because it just wasn't there.

"There it is! Do you hear it?" I let out a small breath and then held it again, so I could hear. "It's around 156 beats per minute, which is perfect!" She grinned at me. I realized I had a death grip around Brian's hand, and I slowly released.

My tears turned to sobs as Brian pulled out his phone to record for a minute. "I'll just hold it right here for a minute, so you can listen," the nurse said. "Then we'll get you on your way home."

***

Christmas Eve dinner was always a very intimate occasion. Brian and I both had small families, so Christmas Eve was usually spent with Brian's mom and grandma. Even so, the thought of Christmas was so horrifying to me this year that I spent most of the day in bed, crippled with sadness. Reluctantly, we headed to my mother-in-law's.

I was anxious even before I sat down at the dinner table. I just wanted it over with. Honestly, I don't think anyone really wanted to be there. We were just going through the motions. As soon as we started eating, Brian's grandma asked, "Did you get that Christmas card from the Millers? Oh, those triplets. You know, back when I was a kid nobody had more than one baby at a time. It's incredible to see three babies, all of them identical! Did you see that?"

My cheeks and ears burned, and my anxiety and grief and anger erupted inside of me. I had always managed to keep it together in front of Brian's family, but tonight, Christmas Eve, it wasn't going to happen. "No," I half-yelled. "No, I didn't see it because I don't open Christmas cards anymore. I don't open them because they might have babies on them. Most of them do. Or baby announcements—From the Smith family: Jacob, Annie, Stella, and Baby #2! And especially BECAUSE I MIGHT SEE TRIPLETS!" I whipped my napkin down on my plate and ran into my mother-in-law's bedroom, slamming the door behind me.

As soon as I was in there, I didn't know what to do. The last time I had thrown a giant tantrum and run out of the room, I had been in middle school. I threw myself on the bed, my chest heaving in and out, the tears coming so freely. I fumbled for my phone to text Bree.

> I'm stuck in my mother-in-law's bedroom, and I'm not quite sure what do. So I texted you, because . . . can you tell me what I'm supposed to do now?

> Why are you stuck in your mother-in-law's bedroom?

At that question, something triggered inside of me. All of a sudden, this became hysterically funny to me. I let out a giggle, followed by a wave of laughter. I texted back,

> I ran away from the table . . . because they were talking about triplets!

I finished typing and laughed, doubling over onto the bed.

> I ran away like a three-year-old, and now I'm stuck in a bedroom, and I don't know how to go back out!

Her reply took a minute.

> You've got this. Just go back out there and say you have severe, explosive diarrhea, and you need to go home. Go home, put on your pajamas, and watch a Christmas movie. You've got this.

I calmed myself down and stood in the doorway, doing a little self-talk. *You've got this!* But as I walked into the hallway, I could hear Brian's grandma talking. "Well, what did I do? What is she so mad about? For God's sake, she's got to move on. These things happen. They happened a lot in my day. Sometimes the baby just isn't right, and so there is a miscarriage. It's time to move on."

A million thoughts swirled in my head. *I didn't have a miscarriage! There was nothing wrong with my babies. It was ME! I was the broken one! It doesn't just happen. And I can't move on. How could I? If you had seen them . . . if you had met them. If you only knew.*

Just the year before at Christmas, we had told our families that we were pregnant. We didn't know there were two babies until New Year's, but I had this memory of standing in the kitchen of our house, peeling potatoes for Christmas dinner, watching Brian put the gifts under the tree, knowing that in one of those gifts was a baby bib for his mom.

My father-in-law had just died, and everyone was so sad. A new baby, we all thought, would help us muddle through our nasty grief. There had been so much happiness. I had also been so sick. I had morning sickness morning, noon, and night. I wore sea-sickness wristbands and sucked on those special morning sickness suckers, but the only thing that really helped was when I ate graham crackers.

We told everyone about our pregnancy way before I was out of the first trimester. I never really believed you should wait. Of course, I didn't really think anything would actually happen to me either.

The holiday season was excruciatingly painful. I would sit in my office, scrolling through Facebook, watching the happiness, while I screamed and cried and slammed my fists on the computer desk. I was so angry at my family because I wanted to be treated like I was fragile. I was broken. I wasn't normal. But they acted like nothing was wrong. Almost everyone did. Brian didn't know what to do with me. Of course, he always hinted that I should maybe think about not logging onto social media quite as often.

There was a picture on a blog once of a Thanksgiving table where the host had set out a place card with the name of the baby who had died, remembering him and holding his place. I was instantly furious and insanely jealous when I saw it. "Nobody has a place at our table for our babies," I wailed. No one had ever had a place card for anyone at our table, but that wasn't the point. Their names weren't even being said. We were all just pretending like they didn't exist, like they never had existed.

Thanksgiving dinner also found me frantically escaping the dinner table. After an uncomfortable conversation about politics, an uncle randomly started bragging about how great of a babysitter his daughter was. "She watches these baby twins," he puffed. "They are so much work, but she does it, every weekend. They are so cute, a boy and a girl, and gosh, you should see them. They are just so chubby and happy . . ."

Never in my life had so many people talked about twins so often. They were everywhere. At the grocery store. In the post office. At the movies. And even though I was secretly growing a new baby, it didn't take one little bit of the sting away. There was so much pain, re-entering life after loss. And while I was grieving, I also had the paralyzing anxiety that came along with this new pregnancy.

I don't think I made it through a holiday meal without either crying or leaving the table for probably two years after the twins were born. A different Thanksgiving dinner, with the other side of the family, sent me into hiding outside of my grandpa's assisted living center, breathless with tears, after my grandpa's wife passed around new baby photos. "These are the pictures of my newest grandbaby. Still waiting for more, Christy and Brian. When are you giving us some grandbabies?"

I know that grandmas pass around pictures of their grandbabies. This is what they do. But it burned me down to my soul that *no one* sitting around that giant table would stick up for me. Couldn't they see? Couldn't they see my pain? I felt like it preceded me everywhere I went, like ominous foreshadowing in a bad novel. The words cut me so deeply, and it was as though the scars should be visible to everyone, not just me. Wasn't it obvious how much pain I was in?

Looking back, I suppose that maybe it wasn't. And truthfully, people just don't know how to handle the pain. We are uncomfortable because we want to fix it. And there is no fixing this grief. There is no distraction, no diversion.

Knowing I had a tiny baby inside didn't stop my constant wondering about what would have been. Two sweet babies in their Christmas best, being passed around as we opened gifts. Matching Christmas footie pajamas and pink and blue packages stacked under the tree. A picture in front of our stockings with Brian holding one baby and me holding the other.

After the blur of the holidays was over, my life settled into a routine of anxiety and stress, on top of my normal grief. I didn't sleep for at least three nights leading up to my first official doctor appointment after I graduated from the fertility clinic. What would my cervix look like? Would it be long enough, whatever that really meant? Would there be a heartbeat?

Driving in the car on the way to the clinic, I started thinking about my anatomy ultrasound with the twins. The technician had recorded a DVD of the ultrasound so that we could watch it later. The first disk the technician tried kept popping out, and she realized that it hadn't recorded our appointment. So she grabbed a new one and restarted the system and did a quick viewing so we would have something recorded. When we arrived at my mother-in-law's house to tell her the news about the babies being a boy and a girl, we popped in the DVD to find it didn't work.

Was that a sign? Did I believe in signs? I remember feeling a deep, dark twinge when that DVD didn't work. I ignored it, pushed it away, because that was ridiculous. But now, on the way to this appointment, I realized I didn't want the doctor to use anything that could malfunction.

I would need to watch for signs in this pregnancy, I decided. I had clearly missed obvious signs that the babies were going to die. The week before my water broke, I had a long phone conversation with my mom about my sister who was stillborn. I had asked her all of the questions I had wondered as a child. Why did the baby die? What was it like to come home? What had happened to the nursery?

That was a *week* before my water broke. That couldn't be coincidence, could it? It was like life was letting me know, "Hey, this same thing is going to happen to you, so listen to your mom's advice and get ready."

On this particular afternoon, I had to go to my appointment alone. I had assured Brian several times that I would be "just fine." Neither of us really had any time off because of all the days we had used with the twins, and I also really wanted him to be able to save the few days he had to be with the baby when he or she was (hopefully) born. Besides, this appointment was only a check-up, and we had just heard the heartbeat, so I knew everything was (hopefully) just fine. This would be quick. In and out. (Hopefully.)

The moment I sat down in the waiting room, I could feel the panic creeping in. First, my leg started to shake. Next, my cheeks started burning hot and red. My heart started pounding as if I had just finished a cardio workout. My thoughts began to swirl around. Words pounded into my temples. *Dead. Dead. Dead. You never can trust a second twin. It's time that you guys look at this funeral home brochure. They would have been serial killers anyway. It was all part of the plan, all along. You'll be grateful someday.*

By the time it was my turn, I knew this baby was dead, too. If it wasn't dead now, it would be soon. My body couldn't do this. What the hell had I been thinking? I walked into the exam room, practicing what I would say. "Oh, it's okay. I understand," I would reply. "I knew I wouldn't be able to do this. I won't do it again, I promise."

There was a nurse standing there. She took one look at me and motioned for me to sit down. "Let's take your blood pressure after the appointment is over. We'll need a urine sample then, too. Let's get this ultrasound over with first."

Once I was in a gown and scooted all the way to the end of the table, she said, "The doctor will be here in a moment, so let's get ready. Have you had a trans-vaginal before?"

I nodded.

"Okay, good. We'll get it over with as quickly as we can. I'm putting this rubber protectant over the wand and then adding some jelly. We'll measure your cervix and look for a strong heartbeat."

I nodded again.

At that moment, there was a short, quick knock on the door, and the doctor walked in. My insides froze.

"Well, good afternoon, Christine. Let's see. Oh, yes. That's right. Okay. Let's check things out. Go ahead, nurse."

She inserted the wand and began to search. Right away, I saw the baby. *It's dead*, I thought. *Oh my God. I don't see any heartbeat at all.* It just kinda looked like it was floating there. I couldn't hear anything. *Fuck. I knew it. I knew it.*

"Oh, oops, I don't have the sound on!" the nurse chuckled. "Hold on here." Suddenly, warmth flooded my body. "Here's the heartbeat, right here," she said. She indicated on the screen where I should look.

"Okay, great, but we're not here for a heartbeat check today. Let's see the cervix," the doctor directed, irritated. She moved the wand a little and did some clicking on the keyboard.

"There it is," the tech pointed.

"Move over," the doctor demanded. "This isn't right. You need to get it exactly at the beginning and end." He pushed his way across me and grabbed the computer mouse. He clicked again.

"There," he said. "That measurement is just fine. You're just past the first trimester, though, so usually they don't budge much then. We'll be checking every week until twenty-four weeks to make sure nothing's moving. See you next time." He got up and walked toward the door.

"Wait!" I yelled. *Did I just yell?*

He turned and looked.

"What was the measurement? I mean, what does "fine" mean? Is it average? Less than average?" I really couldn't believe I still had a wand up my vagina, and I was questioning the perinatologist.

"4.5 cm. It's the *longest* cervix there ever was. Way, way above average, Christine. Now, I have to be going. Have a good day."

I looked over at the technician, letting out all the air I had sucked in. "I think he likes you," she said, smiling. "Now, let's go back and quick hear that heartbeat again."

Each week I had an ultrasound, and my cervix would be "way, way above average" or "the longest cervix you have ever seen." After each appointment, I would feel a huge sense of relief. I had made it one more week. But the relief would always be short-lived, and in the back of my mind the bigger deal was that I was approaching twenty-one weeks, the gestation when my water broke.

Around week nineteen, my night terrors were keeping me up so much that I was barely able to function at work. During the day, I snapped at people at school. In the evenings, I took it all out on Brian or freaked out at my mom over the phone. I didn't want to talk about being pregnant. But then again, I did. Bree would tell me, "You need to remember to enjoy this. Not everyone gets to be pregnant. Let it make you happy."

But the fear just made that really hard. I felt paralyzed, like I was just stuck somewhere, frozen, waiting for something bad to happen. I emailed my grief counselor, but this wasn't grief. It wasn't anxiety. It was straight-up terror.

I was so desperate that I looked online to see if anyone had advice about how to sleep. I didn't want to take any medication. My pregnancy was fraught enough; I didn't need to add on worrying about what category my medication was in. Somewhere, maybe on a blog, I saw a link to a hypnosis CD. It was called something like, "Baby, Stay In!" and was a relaxation and sleep hypnosis CD that was specifically made for women suffering preterm labor or complications. Without giving it too much thought, I clicked "Purchase."

Once I had the CD in my hand, though, I had some second thoughts. It just felt so weird. I had always made fun of the people at the county fair who had paid for hypnosis to lose weight or quit smoking. It felt so fake, like I was buying snake oil from a sleazy salesman.

But that night, I decided I would go ahead and do it. I waited until at least 9:45 before I went to bed (I was too afraid to be in bed at the time that my water had broken), then I plugged in my ear buds and set my MP3 player carefully next to me.

The woman's voice was very soothing. She assured me that my baby would stay in and that I just needed to breathe in and breathe out. Let my body relax its way to sleep. The baby was going to stay in until he or she was ready to come out. I should think about my cervix staying nice and long and sealed shut. It was not ready to open up and let that baby out. It was staying in.

Was I actually hypnotized? Nope. But, I will admit, it did actually help me fall asleep. Not always, but a lot of the time. I told myself that I was actively doing something that would help my baby—I was relaxing and trying to let my body rest. My brain needed a rest from the non-stop anxiety.

The day that I turned the gestational age of twenty-one weeks and three days, I woke up in a very strange mood. I didn't cry. I didn't rage. I kept telling myself that the chances that I would have the very same thing happen on the very same day in my pregnancy were so slim. I went about my day, and I came home and made dinner. Brian kept looking at me like I was going to break at any moment, but I felt so strangely strong.

What's weird about grief, for me, is that it never quite does what I expect it to. Anxiety doesn't always come with the things you thought you'd be anxious about. I have been obsessed with dates and numbers since the twins died. I purposely never want to know the gestational age of any pregnant woman. I wish I didn't know the chances of survival in the NICU if the baby were born that day.

Once, one of my friends told me that her sister was having serious contractions at twenty-eight weeks. I was so bitter that I quickly retorted, "Twenty-eight weeks? That baby will be fine. Don't even worry about it. Twenty-eight weeks, she's golden." I remember her just staring at me.

I mean, you are certainly *not* "golden" if your baby is born at twenty-eight weeks. Having a baby born at that premature gestation is serious and nothing to be taken lightly. But again, my anger and grief made me feel like everyone else should just have to deal with it. So what? I'd think. At least *your* baby will be alive when it's all done.

Yet when I really expected my fear to be insurmountable, like on this day, I was fine. I have no idea why, really. Maybe the lead up is worse than the actual day? I don't know.

I had this idea that as soon as I hit twenty-three weeks and four days pregnant I would be okay.

I woke up and texted Bree.

> I did it! I made it! 23 + 4!

Instead of a text back, though, my phone rang. It was 6:30 in the morning, so I looked down. The name Bree was flashing on the screen. It was 4:30 a.m. in California! My finger hovered over the "accept call" button. Should I answer it???

The thing is . . . we had never actually spoken on the phone. It is the strangest feeling to feel like you know somebody even though you've only emailed and texted. But at this point in my life, she was one of the only people who I spoke to on a daily basis. Besides Brian, she was the first person I contacted when I needed someone.

But my heart was pounding and my throat got dry at the thought of picking up the phone! *What in the hell, Christy?* I picked it up.

"Hello? Bree? Are you okay?"

"Hi," she whispered. "I'm okay, but I'm in the hospital, and I can't sleep, so I thought I'd call you!"

"Oh-my-gosh-oh-my-gosh, are you okay? What's going on?"

"Well, I'm okay. But my contractions were really bad, and I'm still only twenty-six weeks, so they gave me medicine to stop them. My cerclage is still holding, but I'm definitely having preterm labor. My husband went home to sleep and so I'm just here, awake, and I feel sick to my stomach."

I let all of that sink in. After getting a few more details, I asked, "Does this feel so weird to you?"

"Does what feel weird?"

"Well, you know, talking on the phone!" I grimaced. This was so awkward.

But she just laughed me off. "No, it's not weird, you dork! Hey, say the word 'bag' for me," she ordered.

"Why?" I asked.

"Just do it!"

"Um . . . okay. Bag."

Bree burst out laughing. "Bayag. Baaaayyaaag. You are *so* from Wisconsin."

I laughed, too.

From then on, we tried to call each other at least once a week. We were both pregnant, both nearing the one-year anniversary of the deaths of our babies. It was so easy to talk to her, and it seemed like nothing I could say would phase her.

One night, we were video-chatting using our computers and she said, "I want to see your house!"

Brian coughed from the other room. I peeked out, and he had one eyebrow raised. He started mouthing something to me, but I pretended I didn't hear it and went back to my computer.

"Okay!" I said, grinning. "Here we go!" As I gave her a "tour" of my house, I started thinking about how much I wished she lived closer. How much I wished she could come to the March of Dimes walk and Aiden and Sophie's first birthday party. How I wished we could share our babies with each other in real life!

There were pieces of me that were starting to come back together, little by little. There were, of course, some that would never be back together, never fully healed. And that has to be okay.

However, through all the pain of grief, I had managed to find a beautiful, amazing friendship. This was a friendship that, originally, had started to pull me out of the deepest, darkest places of my brain. And now, it was one that made it possible for me to do more than just survive. I was learning to thrive.

CHAPTER 12 - I CAN'T PACK THEM IN A BOX

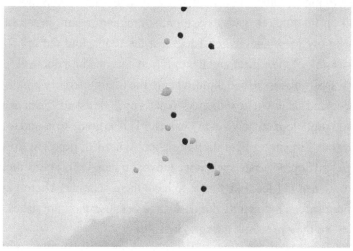

A year. We spent a year counting how many months and days we had survived this world as bereaved parents. Every thirteenth of the month, we had gone to get ice cream in their memory, a pathetic way for us to somehow mark the day. What could we do that would be enough?

Each month that passed felt like such a victory. We survived their due date by escaping to Las Vegas and pretending we were having fun. A distraction, we told ourselves, only there is no way to distract yourself from death. We faked it, celebrating our wedding anniversary with a fancy dinner followed by a good cry. Everywhere we went, all we could think of was how we shouldn't be there. How we should be at home, in a messy house living on coffee and no sleep, changing thirty diapers a day, and getting to know our babies. *Sure, this slot machine is fun, but we should be . . .* was the best we could do.

We faked it. The whole year. We answered, "I'm fine, thanks," when people asked. We smiled and nodded and showed up when we needed to, and then we went home and we waited. Our lives were in such limbo.

At the end of March, we were in the middle of packing up our house to move. Our old house had *finally* sold after eleven months of being on the market. I was six months pregnant again, just past the point in my pregnancy when I had lost the twins, and the upcoming anniversary of their birth and death felt like impending doom.

I was sitting on the bed, holding onto the twins' memory box. Brian came in and sat down next to me. "What's up?" he asked. "You okay?"

Sighing, I looked down at my hands. "This is going to sound totally crazy, but I'm sitting here thinking about what I'm going to do with Aiden and Sophie's ashes when we move. I mean, I can't pack them in a box . . . can I? I feel like I have to have them near me, where I know they are safe. That sounds kinda insane because they are ashes, not babies, so they're totally going to be safe."

"That doesn't sound insane. We won't pack them. We'll keep them with us," Brian replied, putting his hand on my shoulder. "This is not a big deal. *This* we can handle."

"But, babe," I protested, "we will be staying the night at our friends' house after we pack everything up in the truck until the next morning when we close at the bank. Will they freak out when we walk in with our pillow and suitcase and URNS? What the hell? I don't want her to think we've totally lost it. Should I email her about this and make sure she understands? Or is that just going to call attention to it when they may not even notice it at all?"

"Well, we'll just have to put them inside our suitcase so they'll never even have to know. It'll be okay. We've got this."

As I continued to pack up our bedroom, I wondered if we were doing the right thing. I had been so overcome with terrible memories that the moment we arrived home from the hospital, I knew I wanted to put our house up for sale. I hated every square inch of it. I hated going home, and I had done everything I could possibly do to change it, short of a total remodel—of a practically new house.

But now, as everything was coming to fruition, I suddenly had my doubts. A blog friend of mine had said that she would never move because that was the only house where she had memories of her baby. Should I feel like that, too? Was I making a hasty decision?

My mind wandered back to the approaching anniversary of Aiden and Sophie's birth and death. After spending all year wishing for this day to pass, it hit me that I had unrealistic expectations about what this day would mean. It's not like the calendar would turn to April 15th, and suddenly I would feel better—that I'd think, *It's been a year, I'll be good now!* I felt a pressure to celebrate them, to honor their memory, to commemorate their short lives. The pressure was only coming from me, but it was still there, my burden weighing on my shoulders.

What would we do? What *should* we do? I had grown up knowing that my sister, Mary, had been stillborn, but we didn't really talk about it. Every year, on April 2nd, my mom went to put flowers on her grave, but she almost always went alone. I think she preferred that. The twins didn't have a grave for us to visit. Should they have one, I wondered? Did I mess something else up?

On the other hand, I had a blog friend who had a giant birthday party for her baby. It was complete with her entire family and all her friends, balloons, and a three-tiered cake. She planned it like she would have planned a first birthday party for a living baby. Her family seemed so supportive and willing, though. I remembered seeing their picture from Thanksgiving where they had saved her baby a seat at the table. What would I do if I planned everything, and no one showed up?

Bree had donated footprint kits to the hospital, and other moms I knew had even started organizations where they would collect small blankets or wedding dresses to be made into tiny gowns or memory boxes and donated to their local NICU. I wanted to give back, too. I had casts of both Sophie and Aiden's feet and hands, as well as certificates with prints of their feet. They were invaluable to me, and while I hadn't thought about it at the time, now I realized that someone just like us had donated them. Grief had changed me so much, though. I had no energy to start a formal charity organization. Everything just felt so hard.

Initially, the most appealing plan to me was to do nothing. Pretend like it was any other day and speed on through. With no expectations, there could be no disappointments. I wanted this more than anything. I had read blogs of women who did this, and I was sort of jealous. But, it wasn't for me. It *has* to be "whatever works for you." Celebrations and ways to honor your loved one are great—but only if they actually bring you some peace.

When it came time for their first birthday, though, I ended up inviting everyone I knew to come and do a walk for charity with us. It was a walk to raise awareness and money for a big organization that funds research for premature birth. I ordered butterflies to be released, cooked a huge lunch, and raised over $2,000, making us the top money-raising family team. I designed and ordered T-shirts for everybody, with "Team Wopat" printed on the front and two butterflies on the back. I picked up dozens of pink and blue balloons to send off into the sky. Brian and I each wrote a letter to Sophie and Aiden, and we sealed them and put them in their box.

And you know what? Not one of those things mattered to me. They felt forced, like I was putting on a show of what I thought I should do. But, mostly, they were all overshadowed by pain and bitterness. I was *so* angry and resentful that some members of my immediate family couldn't be bothered to even send a text, let alone donate $5 in Sophie and Aiden's name. I spent the day bothered by who wasn't there, instead of grateful for who was. I slammed doors and cried and whined and checked my phone over and over and typed and deleted passive aggressive texts.

Most of our guests were uncomfortable and worried about saying the wrong thing. I was pretty pregnant and scared to over-exert myself on the three-mile walk, so I had rented a wheelchair and needed someone to push me. The course was on a muddy trail, and every bump I went over, I feared that my water would break. I was a disaster.

There were parts of the day that were beautiful, of course. I love looking back at the pictures now and seeing those beautiful butterflies released in their memory. Most of the people who showed up that day continue to "show up" for me, in plenty of other ways. It's taken me such a long time to learn that yes, the dates are important. And if you love someone who is grieving, for real, take out your calendar and write down the days that matter. Record the birthday, the day they died, maybe their wedding anniversary date. And text them. Call them. Write on their Facebook wall. All you have to say is, "Remembering with you today." Give them a hug when you see them. You won't break them. You'll help them heal in all those already broken places.

I also think it's important to tell people what you need. I wrote all over Facebook. Things like, "I am so sad and scared about tomorrow,

APRIL 13TH! YOU KNOW? THE DAY AIDEN AND SOPHIE
WERE BORN? REMEMBER????" I didn't exactly come right out
and say, "Dear family, please text me tomorrow so I don't feel like
I'm alone in this," but I'm sure they got the drift—well, most of them.

Over the years, I have basically had to lower my expectations. I
know that some of my family members won't call or text or even hit
"like." I have to be okay with that because if I'm not, it just ends up
hurting me. I try to let it help me be a better friend and family member.
I am *so* not perfect. We all do things wrong in our relationships. I
try hard not to harbor resentment, and when the opportunity arises to
share the fact that I am remembering Sophie and Aiden, I take it.

Losing an infant is such a different kind of grief because the things
that we do to honor and remember our loved ones are so hard to do
when nobody else knew them. And if I'm honest, I didn't know them
either. I mean, how well could I know my babies who I only saw for a
matter of minutes before their souls fluttered away? I could love them
more than any other thing on this planet, but I didn't really know them.
I wanted to. I wish I did. I knew a little. They had a life, and they have
a story. But, the rest, we lost. And so I couldn't throw a luncheon after
a funeral where everyone ate lots of food and told stories about how
funny and great and strong they were. And when I say something like,
"I wonder what it would be like to be planning a twin eight-year-old
birthday party," what, really, can somebody say?

Remembering them is almost the only thing I can still do as a mom
for babies who are dead. I want their names whispered into the universe.
I want people to think of them when they hear the word twins. That
isn't too much to ask. And even if it makes people uncomfortable, I'd
like to think they could fake their way through it anyway.

The second year, I planned to do the walk again. This time, after
raising so much money the first year, the organization asked me to
be the sponsored family team and write a speech. I labored over that
speech. I poured my guts into it. I practiced and practiced and couldn't

get through it even once without crying.

The night before the walk, my best friends from college arrived. "Hey! Sarah! Jul! You gotta listen to me! I can do this without crying!" I bragged. As I started in, my face got hot, and the tears started streaming down my cheeks. Soon everyone was crying. I had that totally unrealistic expectation, this mounting pressure that I was putting on myself to be "okay." To be better. To be able to share why I was raising money for this organization without being upset about it.

My children DIED. They were babies, yes. But they were my children. And I will not apologize for being sad about this. I am living a beautiful life, a messy one, sure, but still beautiful. And as long as I am showing up and doing what I need to do, so what if I still cry genuine tears of sadness at the thought of what we are all missing out on. Two beautiful people that, sure, could have been serial killers (thank you again for that), but most likely would have had amazing lives.

When we arrived at the walk, though, it was beginning to rain. Suddenly, everyone was taking down tables and equipment. And the next thing I knew, they were holding the walk in a parking garage. We were walking around in a parking garage. For three miles? My anger seemed to grow and grow as we walked round and round. How was this doing anyone any good? Were we raising awareness? Who even knew we were here? I could go walk around with my friends somewhere else—anywhere else but here. I fumed as we finished, and we moved almost silently into a circle at the end.

I clutched my speech in my hand and could feel the bile rising up, ready to squeeze out. My knees started to shake, and leaning over, I whispered to Brian, "I can't do this. I'm not ready." He looked at me and grabbed my hand without saying a word. I could see the event coordinator was finishing up her speech, and I knew I would be next. I closed my eyes and wished for strength.

And then . . . it was over. People were leaving. And she didn't even call me up there. I looked around, thinking I had missed an announcement to go to a different place, but people were packing up strollers and walking to cars. I looked down at my sweet Avery, her chubby nine-month-old face looking at me from her stroller, thinking about how much I wanted to make her proud. How badly I wanted to share my thoughts and feelings with this crowd of people who were like me.

My friends and family looked to me, not sure what to do. I had told them all about my speech, and then there we were. No speech. There were so many emotions flowing through me, a virtual tornado hurtling emotional debris everywhere, and I wasn't even sure I knew what to feel. Without saying anything, I turned and joined everyone else in packing up our stuff to leave.

Fatigue, embarrassment, the sadness of another anniversary—they all took their toll on me. And somehow, at some point in that mess of emotions, I decided that from then on, whatever I decided to do, that would be enough. If planning this walk and cookout and inviting friends and raising money—if, in the end, it just made me feel empty inside and let down, then what was the point?

Please don't misunderstand—raising money for charity is, of course, something we all should take part in, and I continue to help in this effort. What I mean is that all of the expectations were too much for me. I knew there would be people I would invite to the walk who wouldn't show up, and then I would suddenly feel animosity towards them. When I let myself hope that others would step up and show up, the letdown would break me all over again.

Since then, I have remembered and honored Aiden and Sophie in many ways. Sure, I post things from time to time on social media, but mostly I try to let Sophie and Aiden's short lives impact the way I live my life. I look at the world differently now. I know I am a survivor. I know I am strong. This is all because of their existence. Their short little lives.

I want to be upfront here; the first few years I did a lot on their birthday, and then I realized as the time went on, the planning stressed me out, and it was painful to know that other people didn't remember with me. And so I stopped trying. We always remember Sophie and Aiden. Always. But the days of parties and balloon launches and custom birthday cakes and butterfly releases are in our past.

As an educator, I tell my students about them. I use their story to help my students realize that everyone has hurt and that you can still be okay, even after. I show my fourth graders about how I am using my experiences to help me write a book and that they should, too.

I speak their names into the universe, and I think of them every single day. Every day. Without exception. The good news is, after seven years, when I think of them, it feels peaceful. That may sound strange, but it does. I feel love and peace. Longing, too. Always longing. But most of the time that horrible, gut-wrenching ache that leaves me breathless isn't there anymore. It still comes sometimes, that giant wave of grief, but it washes away when it's done, leaving me almost grateful for the reminder of my love.

Each year at Christmas, I buy them an ornament for our tree, just like I do for my other children. And when ladies are sitting around at lunch talking about their pregnancies or their deliveries, I include my twins in those topics. "When I was pregnant with the twins," I'll say, "I was so sick that I felt like I would throw up all day long, but I never actually did." I'll say that I have had *both* vaginal deliveries and C-Sections.

I don't get to talk about the funny things they say or do. My husband and I will never get to live out that really expensive prom year we laughed about when we found out there were two babies. But, they will never be forgotten. Not if I can help it.

Chapter 13 - We Need To Talk

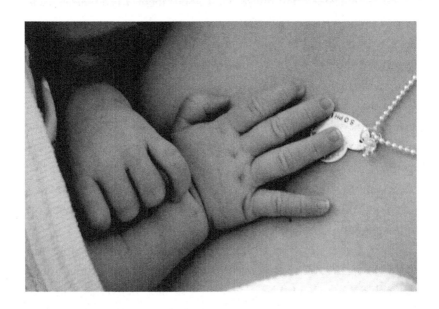

At twenty-eight weeks pregnant, Brian and I had a celebration. We got lottery tickets and went out to dinner, and I wrote a huge blog post about it. "I made it to twenty-eight weeks!" I screamed to the world. "My baby probably won't die (hopefully)!" I went to a store and bought one single preemie-sized baby outfit. "If she stays in longer," I thought, "I can buy it in a larger size later on. But at least I'll have this in case she comes now."

I showed up to my twenty-eight week appointment with the high-risk doctor with a little spring in my step. I was feeling good; it was the THIRD trimester. I had even picked out a crib and put it in my

Amazon cart, thinking I might buy it if I got to thirty-four weeks and was still pregnant. I decided that today, I was happy, and not even seeing this doctor could get me down!

"Hello! I'm twenty-eight weeks pregnant," I announced, as I walked into the exam room. The nurse smiled. "I see that! So, first of all today we need to have you drink this liquid. You have two flavor choices, orange or fruit punch. This is to test for gestational diabetes. You have eight minutes to chug it down, then you need to sit for an hour. We can quickly do your cervical measurement, and then we'll draw your blood downstairs."

So I sat and chugged the orange drink and then got ready for the ultrasound. The doctor came in, as quickly as always, sat down on the stool and just waited for the ultrasound to start.

"Still over 4 centimeters," he reported. "How long is Christine's cervix? It's the longest cervix there ever was." He winked at me.

Today, he amused me. "Oh, thank you for the update. I am SO glad to know it's the longest cervix there ever was!"

He looked around for another minute, then pulled off his gloves and tossed them in the trash.

"So, Christine, we need to talk," he said, pushing his chair over so that he was sitting knee to knee with me.

My heart started to pound. *Fuck*. What had he seen in that ultrasound? I knew it wouldn't be this easy. I wasn't having preterm labor, but my baby probably had a terminal illness. I shouldn't have put that stupid crib in my Amazon cart. I had ruined it. What was I thinking?

"So, the thing is, you are twenty-eight weeks along now, and there isn't a single sign of any kind of preterm labor happening. And there are a lot of women who need a perinatologist to help their babies. So, you're graduating. You don't have to see me anymore. You can go back to a regular OB." He looked at me. Did I detect a little twinkle in his eye? This was not really the time for him to suddenly have charm.

"Um, well, thank you, but no. I'm staying here. I need weekly checks! I need these ultrasounds. I am high-risk!" My voice was borderline a screech. I could feel myself losing control. Tears sprang to my eyes, and I steadied myself on the edge of the examination table.

"Respectfully, you don't need me anymore. And there a lot of women who do. You are going to be just fine. Whatever it was that happened before, it's not happening again. You have a singleton pregnancy, and that sometimes makes all the difference in the world. Good luck." Without waiting for an answer, he walked out. So typical.

I looked at the nurse, still with her hand on the ultrasound machine. I burst into tears, sobbing so hard I couldn't breathe. "I don't want to be graduated," I explained. She just nodded and left the room.

When I got home, I called Brian right away. Unlike me, he was super excited that we were done with the peri. "This is so great! I hate that place. And I don't really like the doctor much, either; he always makes you cry."

That night, I drew myself a bath, as I did every night. It had become a ritual, a sort of healing therapy every night. Sometimes, lying there, with my belly sticking way up over the water, the baby would make huge movements that would send thrills through me. Twelve weeks. Three more months until I would (hopefully) have a living baby in my arms. Time was eternity, and it was nothing at all. How long had it been since I had started yearning for this?

My thoughts were interrupted by my cell phone ringing. I looked over to see the number of the clinic pop up on the screen. "Hello?"

"Hi, is this Christine Wopat?"

"This is she."

"Hi, this is Betsy from the clinic. I'm calling to let you know that you failed the gestational diabetes test we did today. We need to schedule a time for you to come in for the three-hour-long test. You will drink the orange drink, and then you'll get your blood drawn after one hour, two hours, and three hours. This happens a lot, so I don't want you to worry. Can you call the lab tomorrow and schedule your appointment?"

I hung up the phone and settled back into the water, which had turned cold. Gestational diabetes? What even was that? I felt that familiar sense of dread coming over me as I quickly dressed and went to Google. Wikipedia quickly informed me that:

Gestational diabetes, *also known as* **gestational diabetes mellitus (GDM),** *is when a woman without diabetes develops high blood sugar levels during pregnancy. Gestational diabetes generally results in few symptoms; however, it does increase the risk of preeclampsia, depression, and requiring a Caesarean section. Babies born to mothers with poorly treated gestational diabetes are at increased risk of being too large, having low blood sugar after birth, and jaundice. If untreated, it can also result in a stillbirth. Long term, children are at higher risk of being overweight and developing type 2 diabetes.*

If untreated, it can also result in a stillbirth.

Of course it can. Of course it *fucking* can! At that moment, I had no doubt that the test would show I had it. Why wouldn't I have it?

When the nurse called me back a few days after I took the second test, she acted like she was telling me someone had already died. "I'm really, really sorry to tell you this. This really hardly ever happens, honey, but you did fail the blood glucose test. The doctor says you failed two but passed one, so you were close, but unfortunately they just changed the requirements to pass. Since you are so borderline, he wants you to just watch how many carbs you are eating and try to walk each day. I'm really sorry, again."

I hadn't even told Brian anything about it. Should I worry him? Wasn't I doing enough worrying for the both of us? But now, I'd have to tell him.

I had an appointment already scheduled the next day with an OB. Brian was going with me because he knew I was extra nervous. I couldn't get an appointment with my family doctor who I loved, and so I had landed in an OB's office.

A nurse walked briskly in, tapped something on the computer, and told me she needed to take my blood pressure. "Actually," I started, "could we please wait until the appointment is over to do that? Mine is always high until I hear the heartbeat and know everything is okay."

"*Actually*, no I can't," she snapped. "And anyway, there is no such thing as white coat syndrome when it comes to blood pressure. Your blood pressure is high because you are overweight and pregnant."

I looked to Brian. I wanted out. He squeezed my arm, telling me with his eyes that it didn't matter.

"134 over 82. Definitely high. I'll let the doctor know." She walked out.

What was happening? Was I just being sensitive? I tried to take some deep breaths, but I was so fragile. Always teetering on the edge of a giant chasm, ready to fall.

"Hello, Christine, I'm Dr. Collin. It looks like you're transitioning from the high-risk part of our clinic to finish out your pregnancy. Although, it says here that you were just diagnosed with gestational diabetes. This is a concern for me. I'm wondering why they still released you. I'm surprised they wouldn't keep you high-risk after that."

I was kind of shocked. I replied, "Well, the nurse told me that I was just borderline and almost passed. So maybe it's not really that bad?"

Dr. Collins looked at me sharply. "Borderline doesn't exist when it comes to gestational diabetes. You need to take this *seriously*. If not properly managed, babies can *die*. They can be *stillborn*. You'll need to get a blood sugar testing kit and lancets and test your blood sugar 4-6 times a day."

I looked down at the floor as the tears stung my eyes. *Don't cry, Christy. You've got this. You can find a different OB. Don't cry.*

The doctor pushed a button, and a nurse showed up at the door seconds later. "Can you please go get Beth? I'll start the exam in the meantime."

Tears kept falling as I got up on the exam table. She got out the measuring tape, "Hmmm, you are measuring a little big for gestational age."

Moments later a petite, overly-tanned, platinum blonde woman in stiletto heels walked in. She came over to the table and took my hand. "Hello, sweet Christine. Sweet, sweet girl. I can see you are *so upset*. Are things just *really, really hard* right now?"

What. The. Fuck.

"Well, my name is Bethany and I am the hospital's patient *liaison*, and I'm just here because I think you should know that we have a lot *resources* for people who feel *like you do*."

"Feel like I do?" I questioned.

"Yes, honey. I can see you are *so, so upset* right now. And so we want to make sure that you and the baby are staying healthy in *all the ways* a person can be healthy. Physically, you know, and *emotionally*."

I sat up. "Excuse me. But I need to use the restroom. Brian, come on."

I grabbed our coats, and he followed me out of the exam room. "What are we doing?" he whispered.

"We're leaving," I said. I raced out of that hospital. Once I got in the car, I buried my head in my hands. "I cannot believe we just got that lady called on us like we are CRAZY," I said. I didn't know if I should cry or laugh. My insides hurt from anxiety and anger and sadness.

Brian was furious. I don't think, in all my years of knowing him, I have ever seen him that mad. He was cursing, raving. "What the HELL? You cry because they tell you your next baby could die, too, and they go and send you the lady that basically thinks you need to go to the psych ward? OUR BABIES DIED! THEY FUCKING DIED! What do people want from us? How do you not cry?"

We hugged each other tight that day, and after an hour or so, I texted my old doctor.

> Dr. Brown, please, please take me back. I can't go to another doctor. What should I do? Where should I go?

She replied immediately.

> Duh! Of course you should be with me. Call the nurse line and have her schedule you ASAP. See you soon.

For two or three nights, I wallowed in self-pity about my diagnosis with gestational diabetes. I did my usual: Google, try to deny, avoid, and then cry. Then repeat the whole process. Once I got myself together and met with the diabetes educator, I realized it wasn't going to be so bad.

Basically, I had to carefully count carbohydrates and then test my blood about an hour after I ate. I had to keep it under control with food and exercise; otherwise, I would need medication or even insulin. There was a big learning curve in the beginning. Eating a piece of bread would spike my blood sugar higher than a candy bar would. If I did a brisk twenty-minute walk immediately after I ate, it would come down by several points. Luckily, after being extremely regimented, it looked like I could skip medication. The risk of the baby being born with high or low blood sugar would be less because of that.

Around thirty-four weeks pregnant, I began to finally relax about this baby being born prematurely. I stopped my nightly hypnosis and put away my preemie onesies.

Instead, I moved onto being 100 percent certain that my baby would be stillborn. After all, I had gestational diabetes, which increased the chances. And since I always seemed to fall into the one percent, I was sure this was our fate.

One night, Brian came into our bedroom, and I was lying on the bed, crying, with a pad of paper and pen sitting next to me. "What's going on? Why didn't you yell for me? What is this?" He picked up the pad of paper, which was blank. "There's nothing on here!"

I struggled to get a breath. "The baby is dead. I'm supposed to lie here and concentrate on her movements and make tally marks until I feel her move ten times, and it's been an hour and I haven't even felt one. I thought she was asleep, but I just Googled it, and this website says most babies will complete ten movements in about thirty minutes, and so now I just think it's over. I'm not going to the hospital, though. I'm not. Because I am not ready for this. I'm keeping this baby inside for as long as I can. I'm just going to pretend like I don't know. I'm not ready." I felt like my head was exploding.

Brian sat down next to me. "I'm sure she's sleeping. Is there a way we can wake her up so you can calm down?"

I hiccuped. "I could drink juice or something sugary. But I CANNOT drink juice because I currently have DIABETES and so there is NOTHING I CAN DO!" I was wailing now. I threw myself down on the bed, and as I did I felt a familiar little jab, down low by my pelvis.

My heart started pounding. I was always fearful that the baby would kick and make my water break because I had had the sensation of a kick or a punch before Sophie's water broke.

An hour later, my notepad had sixteen tally marks on it, and I was finally calming down. It seemed like every day brought some kind of terrifying event for me. Pregnancy has so many random symptoms and side effects, but for me, anytime something went even slightly wrong, my brain would immediately jump to "This is the end. It's over." I stressed at all times. I was living in "fight or flight" mode, non-stop.

As I neared the end of my pregnancy, and I grew bigger, people would poke fun at my belly. "Are you *sure* you're not having twins?"

was every stranger's go-to quip. As if that isn't annoying enough to any pregnant woman, it is not what a pregnant woman who wishes more than anything she was still pregnant with twins because hers died wants to hear at all. Not even a little bit!

As I neared forty weeks, I just couldn't believe that I was still pregnant. It wasn't lost on me that I had delivered so extremely prematurely, and now it looked like I was going to go overdue. I texted Dr. Brown.

> Please, please, don't let me go past forty weeks. I can't take it!

> Come in for an ultrasound today! See you this afternoon.

Of course, I had read something online and heard from my fellow loss moms that going past forty weeks would also increase my chances of stillbirth. I felt like I just needed to get her out so that she would live.

The ultrasound showed that my baby was estimated to be quite large. Coupled with my gestational diabetes, I was offered a C-Section. Trying to deliver such a big baby could have complications, they told me, and I could end up needing a C-Section anyway. This way I could schedule it and know what was happening in advance.

I hadn't taken the labor and delivery class. I was too traumatized to even let myself think about it. There was no way I could have gone to that class with all the excited first-time parents and NOT be thinking about the fact that I had already been through labor and delivery. I was in some weird, in-between phase where I wasn't a first-time mom, except I was.

I didn't really tell anyone except our moms and a few really close friends that I was opting for a C-Section. I really just wanted to do this on our own, and I had seen enough to know that people would judge me for having an optional surgery when I could have tried to deliver on my own. The choice for me was easy. The anxiety about laboring and delivering when I had read so many awful stories about birth injuries and lost oxygen and lost heartbeats, and my underlying expectation that this baby would never come home with us, felt insurmountable to me. Since there was a medical justification, and since I was completely full-term, I planned my surgery. It would be on July 10th, 2010, eleven months after Sophie and Aiden's due date, and this baby's actual due date.

We needed to be checked into labor and delivery by 5:30 in the morning. At 1:30 a.m., Brian and I were lying awake on our bed, my bag packed and sitting next to the door. We had turned off the TV at midnight, willing ourselves to go to sleep, but it hadn't worked.

"We really should sleep. We are going to need our rest tomorrow, hopefully, if all goes well," I said.

"I just can't really even fathom what's going to happen tomorrow," Brian said. "Our whole lives are going to change tomorrow. Everything will be different. There won't be just us anymore. I wonder what she'll be like. It's so weird knowing that it's happening in a few hours. I just don't even know what to think right now."

"Well, there's no way I'm going to be able to sleep," I answered. "I keep going back and forth, picturing a baby in my arms, and sometimes she's alive and sometimes she's dead."

Brian sat up straight. "You have to picture her alive, Christy," he snapped. "This is a different story. We have to believe that. YOU have to believe that." Having Brian snap at me was a wake-up call. He was right, of course.

The morning took a thousand years to come. At 4:30, we showered and locked up the house. My mom and mother-in-law would meet us at the hospital later, and we would be away from the house for a few days at least.

After checking into the hospital and some rather uncomfortable pre-surgery procedures (Random nurse shave your pubic hair, anyone? Catheter? SO fun.), my mom kissed me goodbye, and Dr. Brown came in to say hello.

"Good morning! Are you ready?" she smiled and started wheeling my bed out the door. "We're going to head to the operating room right now. We'll get you situated, and then Brian can come in in a few minutes, okay?"

Brian let go of my hand and whispered something to me.

At that moment, my heart felt like someone had squeezed it in a vice. I couldn't catch my breath; it was like someone was standing on my chest and jumping up and down. I remember things swirling a little bit, and I could hear people saying my name, "Christy! Are you okay? Christy?"

I don't know how much time passed, but once I finally could take a deep breath, someone came and told me she could give me a pill to help with my nerves, but it might make me sleepy. I was scared I'd freak out and have to be put under and miss the birth, so I took it.

The OR was freezing, and it was such a strange experience to be awake inside of it. It was cold and sterile, with a pungent cleaning-product smell. In each corner there were nurses or orderlies standing around, everyone dressed in scrubs with masks. They moved in and out, sometimes introducing themselves. The anesthesiologist kept asking me questions. A nurse came and told me she was going to hook up a heart monitor so she could track the baby's heartbeat during the delivery.

She picked up the heartbeat right away, thankfully, and the anesthesiologist came back and started explaining the spinal block he was going to insert. I had an epidural with the twins' delivery, so I didn't think it would be worse than that since I wasn't even feeling any contractions. As I curled up and tried to bend over, the nurse suddenly started frantically moving the heartbeat sensor all around.

I burst into tears, trying to understand why this would happen to me. She was losing the heartbeat, and I was minutes away from delivering. *What a cruel, cruel thing,* I thought. *If there is a God, why would he let me have so much hope and then rip it all away like it was nothing?*

After what felt like 18,000 tries, the spinal was in, and I could lie back down straight. The nurse who was fiddling with the heartbeat monitor had taken the strap totally off and was looking around. I needed to know the truth, so I swallowed and croaked out, "Is the heartbeat gone?"

She looked up at me, surprised. "Oh, no! Of course not! I just couldn't get it in the right place while you were bent over, so I was waiting until you were lying back down straight again. I'll get it right back on!"

At that moment someone opened the door, and Brian came in dressed in his scrubs and funny-looking hat and booties, and tears sprang to my eyes. His entrance reminded me that I could do this, that we had survived the worst, and today was going to be the best.

He sat down next to me and smiled nervously. "How are you doing?" he asked. I couldn't respond because they were starting the surgery, and I felt the weirdest sensation of tugging.

Moments later, I heard Dr. Brown say, "Here she comes!"

My body was wracked with sobs when I saw her. Dr. Brown brought her over, and as she got close, she stretched open her mouth and let out a loud cry. She was telling the world that she was not happy! Brian followed her over to get cleaned up and weighed. As she was being set on my chest, someone rang the bell—another baby had been born.

Avery Elizabeth Wopat was born at 8:40 a.m. on July 10, 2010, weighing eight pounds and six ounces, with near-perfect Apgar scores and healthy, working lungs that could scream for hours.

Holding her close to me was an indescribable feeling. Watching my husband gingerly place our baby in my mom's arms for the first time, it was like nothing I could have imagined. It was hard for me to believe that I wouldn't have to give back this baby I was holding. She could stay with me, right by my side.

We didn't have any guests at first besides our moms. All I wanted was for the three of us to be together. I kept pinching myself—was it for real? We got to stay on the labor and delivery floor and have flowers delivered instead of grieving-parent postcards being taped to our door. We took turns holding her, and our days were spent learning how to change tiny diapers and basically just reveling in her perfection.

I cried when we had to go home. I was scared, but it felt so life-changing. So monumental. I was going to get to start my "after." I sat in the backseat next to Avery all the way home, picturing her life. I would do everything I could to make her life great—including helping her remember her brother and sister. I was now the mom of three.

CHAPTER 14 - IF I DON'T REMEMBER THEM, WHO WILL?

To: breemeg@email.com
Subject: hallucinations
From: christywopat@email.com
Sent: July 24, 2010, 5:14 p.m.

Bree,

So, every time I'm holding Avery, I picture terrible things happening to her. I literally can't put her down. I'm not sleeping at all. Like, when I walk around the corner from my bedroom upstairs, I can picture myself tripping and accidentally dropping her down the stairs, and I panic. At night when she sleeps for a few hours at a time, I have to sleep with my hand next to her to make sure she is breathing. Is it like this with Nora? Are you as scared as I am? Did you know people actually put bumpers in their cribs? They're just asking for their babies to suffocate to death!

Love,
Christy

P.S. Still no breast milk at all. Had appt with lactation today. They had me weigh her, then feed her, then weigh her again to see if there's any milk coming out when she nurses, since I can't get any out through the breast pump. Turns out I'm such a freaking freak that I just didn't even make any breast milk at all. Now she's going to get a bunch of diseases and not have a high IQ, thanks to my broken body! Awesome!

To: christywopat@email.com
Subject: Re://hallucinations
From: breemeg@email.com
Sent: July 24, 2010, 9:43 p.m.

Hi,

Yes. Yes. and Yes. Have you ever heard of the Angel Care Monitor? We just got it for Nora. She won't sleep unless someone is holding her, though, so we haven't been able to use it yet. But it's a breathing sensor for underneath the mattress that will sound an alarm if the baby hasn't taken a breath in a few seconds. You should look into it.

Also, I don't want anyone else to touch her. Do you feel like that? Like, I waited so long to get her that I just want her to be all mine.

Love,
Bree

Sophie and Aiden made me a mother; there is no question about that. But getting to be a mom to Avery, having her here to parent, saved my life. She renewed every sense of joy and hope that had dulled inside of me. I would sit for hours, just staring at her, at the miracle of it all. All of the things that I regretted, that I never got to do with my twins, even before they died, I was sure to do now. How I wish I had kissed them all over. How I wish I had studied each of their tiny fingers and tiny toes and looked closely enough to see whose nose and forehead they had.

She gave all of that back to me. She allowed me to experience what it is like for a baby to snuggle in on your chest and fall asleep. She helped me learn what it feels like for someone to want *only you*. Through her, I experienced tiny yawns and excited squeals and first laughs. I got to choose perfect little tiny outfits that seemed to fit her personality and buy dumb little tennis shoes for her that cost more than shoes I buy for myself even though her feet wouldn't even touch the ground in them.

The littlest things that I had wished for were finally coming true for me. I honestly hadn't believed they would. The day that I got to carry my baby in her infant carrier and wander around the baby section of Target, stopping on the way home to get a coffee, I had tears of gratefulness running down my cheeks the entire time. All of the lingering pain and anger and fear couldn't take away the fact that I had this beautiful baby at home, with me, finally.

This little girl taught me so much about life, about living in the moment and not taking anything in life for granted. She taught me to laugh again, and that it really is okay to be completely full of joy one second and rocked to my core with sadness the next.

She did not, however, replace Sophie and Aiden. It wasn't a matter of, "Oh! Avery is here! I get to have a baby! Now I can forget about all that other stuff and *move on*." But that is pretty much what everyone else expected to happen. I think a lot of people breathed a sigh of relief with me when Avery arrived here safely, and then thought, "Oh, thank goodness, now I can stop hearing about her sadness."

The problem is that sadness was (and is) still very much there. With every milestone that I got to experience with her, the weight was upon me that I had missed out on those milestones with my twins. Every Fourth of July fireworks and visit to Disneyland and day spent baking cookies are days that I had ripped away from me with Sophie and Aiden.

People like to remind me that I should be grateful for what I have. "Don't live in the past, Christy, you have a beautiful child *here on Earth* to be thankful for!"

"BUT!" I want to scream. "BUT! Don't you see? I have a responsibility to be a mom to the ones who aren't here, too! If I don't remember them, who will?"

Being a new mom is freaking hard. There are times when you sit back and wonder, "Is this really what I wanted so badly?" And then that pang of guilt hits, because it's pretty much insane to be complaining about something that you have fought for and desperately wanted for so long.

As if grief in its natural state wasn't difficult enough, add on post-pregnancy hormones and extreme exhaustion, and I was barely making it. It was so isolating to feel so dark and twisty when everyone expected me to be blissfully happy because I *finally* had everything I had ever wanted.

Grief does not just disappear. People cannot just be quickly replaced and then the pain of losing them floats off into the universe, never to be seen again. Doctors were concerned about postpartum depression, but really, there just wasn't a clear-cut way to know the difference between the suffocating feelings of grief and those of PPD. I had learned not to talk much about it.

Going about my life without people catching on was manageable. I could smile and laugh and welcome visitors who were anxious to see the baby. But in the wee hours of the night, rocking Avery back to sleep in the new pink glider rocker, the tears would stream down my face. There was a CD of nursery rhymes that I would play at bedtime, and the third song on the disk was "You are my Sunshine." One of the verses went like this:

The other night dear, as I lay sleeping
I dreamed I held you in my arms
But when I woke, dear, I was mistaken
So I hung my head and I cried.

Each and every time that part came on, I could barely get the words out as I sang along. I squeezed Avery so tight and thanked my lucky stars that I had her, but I don't think I had ever felt my loss so deeply. The tears would come so freely and strongly, and for the first time in my life, I realized that true happiness and utter pain were emotions that could actually be felt simultaneously. Beauty and pain, gifts and loss, the absolute worst and the absolute best.

As the side-effects of the exhaustion that every new mom experiences kicked in, my anxiety went into overdrive. I began to worry about everything, but especially about Brian and Avery.

Anytime Brian went anywhere and took even a minute longer than I estimated, I was positive that he had been in a car accident. I would imagine the entire scene playing out with the police officer coming to my door and telling me, "Ma'am, I hate to tell you this, but your husband is dead." If he had so much as a headache, I was certain he had a brain tumor. While he was at work, I imagined he was telling everyone that his wife was crazy and that he was leaving me.

Really, truly, I thought the anxiety would go away. A self-diagnosis of "situational anxiety" kept me quiet about it to my friends and family. Filling out the mental health "quizzes" at the doctor gave me pause, but I knew being honest would mean medication, and I had this messed up determination that it meant I was a failure if I took it.

I absolutely do NOT think that now. In fact, if I could go back and give my former self advice, I would tell myself to be honest and get medical help when I needed it. Surviving without care is not a sign of strength, and I wish now that I had taken advantage of resources much earlier than I did.

Worrying controlled me. It was attached to me, like a parasite, slowly growing, slowly choking me. My worry presented itself first as major irritability. "UGH. Seriously?" I'd huff and puff as I slammed my stuff on the floor. "I just need ONE COUNTER clean in this house. I just asked you to keep THIS COUNTER clean."

As soon as my fit was over, I would almost immediately be wracked with guilt for yelling, for being ridiculous, and for realizing that my grief had won . . . again. This was a battle I was not made to win.

Along with irritability, I was convinced that either Avery would die of SIDS or I would accidentally do something to hurt her. I imagined I would be feeding her in bed when I was so tired, and I'd imagine myself rolling over on her and smothering her. I was psychotic about making sure she only slept in her bassinette with her breathing monitor on. We had bought the monitor Bree told us about, and it was the only way I could sleep, knowing that if Avery stopped breathing, I would be alerted immediately.

I never put her down, except at bedtime when I absolutely couldn't stay awake anymore. I needed every person who came in my house to wash their hands, or at the very least use hand sanitizer before they touched her. I probably seemed like an annoying, over-protective first-time mom, but in my head I was picturing her in the hospital, dying from influenza. And I knew what watching your baby die was like.

One particular evening, I had been awake with Avery practically all night. None of the normal things were working to soothe her, and she was overtired and just couldn't settle. I sent a series of panicked texts to Bree explaining that I had tried everything either of us could think of to soothe Avery, including a warm sink bath and even driving her around the neighborhood, slowly.

I paced back and forth, bouncing and swinging her around, past my point of desperation, and consumed by fatigue. On one swing, I felt my elbow hit the wall, with her head following closely behind it, *almost* hitting the wall. My mind flashed, and I pictured Avery's tiny, soft little skull slamming against it, thick blood splattering and trickling all the way down. I ran to wake up Brian, sobbing, begging him for help.

Thankfully, he helped, and I never had an experience quite that awful again. I learned to tell Brian that I needed him to take her, and he would just understand, without asking any questions. Even now, years later, I can remember standing in the hallway outside of my classroom at school and admitting this to some ladies I was starting to become friendly with at my new building. Both of them looked at me and said,

"Oh, yes. Of course! Us, too. Exhaustion can do some wicked things, and couple that with hormones? Thank goodness it's only a season." That simple connection gave me so much comfort.

Motherhood is terrifying. You are pushed to the point of absolute desperation. Exhaustion is nothing to mess around with. Of course, at the time, I only had Bree to talk to, and she was going through her first time right along with me. We were both still grieving and going through rough hormonal changes. We didn't know what the hell was going on. Was it normal, what we were experiencing? We were both telling each other the same things, but was it because we were just in the same place?

There are books all about the entire experience of pregnancy, even books that try to tell you what is "normal" for the toddler years or your child's life. There are bloggers who make fun of letting their kids watch too much TV or feeding their kid too much junk food or letting laundry pile up all over the house.

But the really deep, dark stuff? The stuff that you're ashamed to even tell your spouse about? It's not out there. And it happens, even to the very best parents. I have never hurt my children, I've never even thought about hurting them. But I have thought about running away. I have locked myself in a bathroom while my kids pounded on the door, and I sat on the toilet and cried.

I have screamed so loudly and so forcefully that I've scared even myself. I have acted like a pouty, sullen teenager and said things like, "FINE. WHATEVER. DO WHATEVER YOU WANT. I DON'T CARE ANYMORE." When Avery was an infant and nothing would calm her, I had to put her in a crib, shut the door, and leave the room to breathe.

I let myself wonder if I was crazy. I let myself think that I was a terrible mom, and that losing the twins had ruined my life, and that it would make me a lunatic mother. I felt so guilty that I finally had this beautiful, perfect baby, and I couldn't even do it right. People looked at me when I fed her formula—I never, ever got any breast milk, so I didn't even have a choice, but I still felt the guilt. They looked at me when she got older and threw fits. I left stores crying, embarrassed because I felt like the one thing I always wanted to do, and be, I totally sucked at.

My friendships suffered at the hands of my grief. I couldn't even look at anyone who had been pregnant at the same time as me when Sophie and Aiden died. I blocked photos from social media, and if one slipped through, I would cry all day. I only had my blog friends, and I had never even met them in real life. They were the only ones who understood me. We shared our lives on those blog pages, and in turn we were validated and comforted and supported. I continued to blog into the wee hours of the night with Avery sleeping peacefully beside me.

My words, mixed with their comments and their posts, were my saving grace, again, now that our babies were here and alive. We exchanged phone numbers and Facebook pages as we ran out of time for our long blog posts. Alissa from Wisconsin, Angie from Iowa, Sally from Australia, and Angela from Missouri—they all felt like they were sitting next to me, old friends whom I could text about my deepest, darkest worries and fears. Just like always, anything I said was met with, "Oh, yes, me, too."

I remember a night when I had seen a particular pregnancy announcement on Facebook that left me gutted. I went into my room and took out the wooden chest that held the mementos from the twins. Inside are their urns, their hospital bracelets and baptismal gowns, the pictures that the NICU nurses took, and some extra special cards that we've received over the years.

Avery was sleeping next to me in her bassinet, and Brian was gone. I sat on my bed and opened up the box. My ritual was to take each item out one at a time and look it over, holding each one in my hands. I could feel that familiar rage and pain brimming up to the surface, my sobs escaping out once again. The first picture I took out was of Aiden in his isolette, wearing his baptismal gown. Stunned, I looked closer. *Avery looks exactly like him.* My heart broke all over again. I would get to watch Avery change and grow. I would get to see her become a toddler and a teen and a young adult; with luck I would get to see her on her wedding day and then become a grandmother. But Aiden and Sophie would forever be frozen in time—their tiny little features all I would ever remember.

Time stood still as I watched Avery sleep. I couldn't reconcile my emotions. I couldn't make anything fit anymore. Should I be *moving on*, now that I had a daughter to raise? Was I dwelling on the negative, like people said?

Another time I was at a craft fair, and I found these little stones with names engraved on them. I instantly thought they would be perfect for their memory box, so I purchased one that said Sophie and one that said Aiden. I heard one of my friends whisper to another one that it was weird that I didn't buy one that said Avery. Seeing that through their eyes was difficult for me. To me it made perfect sense. I bought things for Avery all the time! I got to dress her and buy her toys and pick out books that she would love. I got to be her mom in so many ways that I didn't get to do for my twins.

As my maternity leave came to an end, I started feeling more and more anxiety thinking about leaving Avery at daycare. Since she had been born in summer, and since I am a teacher, I was able to take the first three months of school off with her, and my husband the next month after that. So, luckily, she was almost six months old before she had to go to daycare. I found an in-home daycare on the same street as me, and I trusted the provider a lot. It had nothing to do with the person watching her, I just felt like if I left her, something very bad would happen (read: she would die).

Of course people would tell me, "It'll be so fine! You'll be back to work for a few days, and it'll be like it's always been that way!" But they didn't have to live inside of my head. They didn't have my night terrors and my anxiety. This wasn't a "normal" mom returning to work after having a baby—and that is hard enough!

A lot of my blog friends were fortunate enough to be able to stay home with their kids. I hadn't even really considered it. I had a great job in an excellent school district, and we needed both of our incomes to keep our house. Suddenly, I was desperate. I scoured job sites and wondered how many kids I would have to watch at my own daycare to make up my salary from work (like 25). I found myself idiotically calling the numbers on those creepy signs that say "Make $500 a week from home! Call this mysterious number from the sign that doesn't tell you anything about what the job actually is and probably involves drugs or porn!"

The first day back was a blur. I was crying by the time I reached my car after leaving her and didn't stop until school started. Thankfully, I had a lot of support at work, and daycare texted me pictures throughout the day to show me that Avery was doing well. My students were an awesome distraction, and before I knew it, eighth hour was over. I flew out of there at the end of the day, leaving a giant pile of work on the middle of my desk. All I cared about, desperately, was getting to her.

After the chaos of the first week calmed, though, I settled into a routine and tried to move forward the best I could. I was counting down the days until summer, already feeling the drain of a working mom's schedule.

A few weeks after my return to work, driving home alone on the interstate late at night, my van hit a patch of black ice. Brian was home with the baby, and I happened to have him on speakerphone as I drove. As soon as I started to spin, I screamed to Brian, "Oh my God. Oh my God!" I slammed on the brakes in an attempt to avoid the cars in front of me which made everything worse, and within a moment I was spinning in my van and catapulting toward a ditch. As the van spun out of control, I held my breath and thought *I am going to die. After all this, I'm dying. And now Avery will not have a mom. I lost my kids, and now Avery will not have a mom. She needs me, and now I am dying.* I dropped the phone in the chaos, but I could hear Brian's voice. "Babe? BABE? What's happening? Oh my God, BABE!" The urgency and shakiness in his voice didn't even register with me. I looked out the window, noticing that I was reaching the edge of the road. *I hope he knows how much I love him.* I couldn't believe that after all this, I was going to die. My baby girl was going to live without a mother, and Brian would be ruined. It was so much like they say, I couldn't believe it. Even though I was spinning quickly, time inched forward at a snail's pace, and I had time to think about the fact that I was going to die.

After catapulting into the snow covered ditch, my van was banged up, and I was physically fine, but emotionally wrecked. I wondered if "normal" people would immediately think that they were going to die like that. Was I now resigned to the fact that I'd think every bad thing would end up as the worst possible outcome? Would this be the way that I'd live my life now? Forever?

There is much to be said about understanding that life is fleeting, that everything can be flipped upside down in a moment. However, this night helped illuminate the fact that I was also still stuck in the trenches of PTSD. My anxiety wasn't getting any better. I didn't want to be someone who expected the worst. There are some people—you know them, too—who just seem to be able to take anything that life hands to them and move forward with optimism. I wanted to be that person, but I just wasn't.

I wonder now if those people really exist, or when alone with their thoughts are they just like me? Do they tell you that all is well, but it's all a front? I guess I've always just tried to be as honest as possible about my feelings, knowing that others hide theirs. Hiding our feelings to look stronger . . . that's what we do, right?

I don't think that feeling, the one where I'm waiting for the other shoe to drop, will ever go away. I know that we are not safe, that lightning can and absolutely does strike twice. I know that any of us, at anytime, could be staring right in the face of tragedy. However, long gone are the days when I looked at the future with only dread. That night, that car accident, it helped me to realize that I needed to pay attention. I needed to believe that everything was going to be okay, even if it wasn't.

After that night, Brian, Avery, and I hardly left our house if we didn't have to. We just basked in the luck and beauty of it all. We read books and binge-watched TV shows. We had each other, and we were going to spend every minute together, remembering the twins, carrying them along with us, but moving forward the best we could.

CHAPTER 15 - CARMAGEDDON

From: breemeg@email.com
Subject: so....
Date: June 19, 2009
To: christywopat@email.com

So, some bad news. The weekend you are coming is the weekend of this crazy traffic closure in LA. We have like 2 major highways and one of them, the 405, is going to have a 10-mile stretch of it closed for 48 hours. They're telling everyone to stay off the roads because they won't be able to get anywhere. So, if you get here on Friday, I could drive to your hotel and we could have lunch and then I'd have to get home quickly. So I would only get to hang with you for about an hour or so.

But . . . and if this is too weird, I understand . . . I could just come and pick you up Friday morning and then bring you back Monday morning once the road is open again. You wouldn't get to stay in the hotel then, and you'd have to trust me that I'm not a creepy old man pretending to be your blog friend.

Let me know what you think! I know it's crazy! But maybe we could see Rachel and Tina, too?

From: christywopat@email.com
Subject: Re: so....
Date: June 19, 2009
To: breemeg@email.com

Wow. OK, so my first question is, does your husband think you are crazy for inviting a stranger to stay the entire weekend?

From: breemeg@email.com
Subject: Re: Re: so....
Date: June 19,2009
To: christywopat@email.com
   I can't say that he jumped up and down and clapped. But, he is OK with it. Did you ask Brian yet

From: christywopat@email.com
Subject: Re: Re: Re: so....
Date: June 19, 2009
To: breemeg@email.com

   He gave me a funny look and a shrug (this is an average response). I feel like I met a new boyfriend on match.com, and I have to make sure we meet in public first to make sure he's not a serial killer. I mean, I know you're you. And I know I'm me. But . . .

   I say, let's do it! I would hate to fly all the way to California and get to see you for one hour because of a traffic jam!

From: breemeg@email.com
Subject: Re: Re: Re: Re: so....
Date: June 19, 2009
To: christywopat@email.com

   They're calling it Carmageddon. They are even selling shirts on the street corner that say *I Survived Carmageddon 2011*. I'm going to get you one!

   I'm so excited now! Wanna Skype with the girls tomorrow?

From: christywopat@email.com
Subject: Re: so....
Date: June 19, 2009
To: breemeg@email.com

OMG. Carmageddon. Seriously. That is awesome. I hope I see a celebrity while I am there. Or at least a Kardashian.

We'll Skype you tomorrow at 5 p.m. my time? Oh, and I am already out of texts, so that's why I'm not replying. Need unlimited texting plan! Talk to you tomorrow!

Brian shrugged his shoulders. "Is this seriously something you want to do? Where will you and Avery sleep? Where does she even live? Maybe just having lunch is the better option here. This feels *very* weird, I have to tell you."

I went to sit right next to him and showed him the article on the computer screen: "Los Angeles Braces for Weekend of 'Carmageddon.'"

"I mean . . . I don't know. I think it's silly for me to sit in a hotel room while you go to your sessions when I could be hanging out with Bree and Nora. Look, I Googled 'Carmageddon,' and it's a real thing. So that's one step closer to thinking we're not going to get kidnapped . . . " I laughed, and turned to look toward him.

He looked me in the eye, not amused. "We have some *actual issues* to think about. We won't have a car there. What happens if you get there and her house is disgusting or her husband is a creeper, and you are miserable? I won't be able to just come and get you. I don't know. This just feels really, really wrong."

I rolled my eyes. "Babe. Her house is in a really cool part of LA. I think it's where all the D-listers live. I might even see a celebrity while I'm there! And they just moved there. I've seen pictures. Her husband is nice, I'm sure, really nice. It's totally going to be fine."

"Christy. You met her *on the internet*. I know it's not 1996, but here is this girl that you text and email and call, and you've never even met her." He grabbed both my hands. "I just want you to know . . . I think you are insane."

I thought for a moment. "Think of it this way," I started. "I have made dinner plans with someone who I only met once or twice or only knew from work. And Bree, I have known her, even if it is just on the internet, for a year and a half. She knows so much about me, and she loves Avery. This is not a real stranger. It's going to be good. Great, even!"

As Brian sighed, he grabbed my hand. "I'm going to trust you on this one. But, I still think there's a chance that Bree is a lonely, sad, sixty-year-old man looking for a girlfriend."

Laughing, I hit him on the shoulder. "Whatever!"

***

Six weeks later, I sat on a hotel room floor, hovering behind Avery. Approaching her first birthday, she could pull herself up to a standing position now and cruise around, knocking things over, and wobbling dangerously around sharp corners.

"Avery," I said. "We're about to go do something really cool today. Pretty special, actually. You and Mama are going to go meet our friends Bree and Nora. They are kinda like our family. They are our people. We're going to have so much fun!"

"Yeah, and Mommy met them on the internet, which is *really* special," Brian added from the corner. I gave him the stink eye.

My phone pinged a text. Bree.

About 10 minutes away!!!!!!!

My stomach dropped and somersaulted. I had been so flippant about it in front of Brian, but now I was kinda sorta freaking out. "Ok, baby Avery! Let's get our bag and your car seat. It's time to go!"

I grabbed Avery and set her on my hip to head out to the elevator. I tugged my shirt down and switched her to the other hip. This time Avery grabbed my head and tousled my hair. Setting her down, I started fussing with my hair. Brian eyed me suspiciously. My nerves had totally set in. Obviously, Bree wouldn't care about my hair or my crumpled shirt.

As the elevator door opened, my phone pinged again.

> **We're here! Out front!**

I took a deep breath and hoisted the diaper bag up onto my shoulder. Avery's legs were wrapped around my hip, her chubby hands squeezed tightly around my neck. I looked straight into her eyes, took a deep breath, and said, "Are you ready for this?" She looked back at me, blankly, having no idea what was really happening.

From behind me, Brian laughed. "I'm fairly sure she's ready for anything. Are *you* ready?"

I nodded and pushed the door open, the hot air instantly wrapping me up like a cocoon. We moved awkwardly out the door, Brian close behind with my suitcase and Avery's car seat. I wished I could hide for a minute. Why was I so nervous?

I looked around for Bree, my mouth dry. Taxis were zooming all around the cul-de-sac in front of the hotel, and people in flowery shirts and sundresses were dragging their piles of luggage out of the trunks. I was distracted momentarily by a couple pushing a double stroller. A quick glance told me they were twins, so I looked away.

Just then, out of the corner of my eye, through a crowd of people, across the hotel's main parking lot, I spotted a flash of red hair.

Holding my breath, I looked closer, knowing instantly that it was her. I watched as she fussed with the car seat strap and then straightened up and pulled out baby Nora. As she turned, I realized I had been holding my breath. At that exact moment, she noticed me, and she looked over and waved, a grin spreading across her face.

After all these months, thousands of texts and emails and phone calls, middle-of the night marathon Facebook messaging sessions, there we were, just a few feet from each other. How many times had I wished I could just meet her for coffee, or go to a movie, or just give her a huge hug to let her know that everyone would be okay? How many times had I just wished that she lived down the street from me and we could sit around and be broken together?

And now, it was happening. Before I knew it she was on her way over to me. We set the girls on the grass, in the shining, warm sun, and we reached for each other. I squeezed with all my might, years' worth of thank-yous all wrapped up into this moment. Years' worth of check-ins and caring for each other and making each other feel normal again. Here she was, my hero, the woman who had saved my life, close enough to finally embrace.

I grabbed a plastic bag from the ground and pulled out the stuffed toys we had gotten the night before. I gave one to each of the girls. They were soft and pink and had a little bell rattling around on the inside. Avery and Nora both still have them all these years later. I'd like to think that someday, hopefully, they'll understand their significance.

Seeing Avery and Nora next to each other stirred up a full range of emotions. From amazement and joy that they were there together, alive and happy, to a deep, deep sense of regret that the only reason we were there was because their siblings died. To this day, there is still a disbelief that they lived. That our bodies, which had let us down in the most horrific way, had brought us these beautiful girls. And there they were, sitting next to each other in the warm California sunshine.

Brian came over and exchanged a slightly awkward 'hello' and hug with Bree. He nervously began to install Avery's car seat in Bree's car and double-checked with her that he had her correct address. "Now, you're sure this is okay with you and your husband?" he asked, suspiciously, as Bree strapped Nora back in.

Laughing, she replied, "We will take good care of her. I swear! It's totally Carmageddon's fault. And at least now you know I'm not a sixty-year-old man looking for a girlfriend, so hopefully you'll be able to sleep easy tonight!" She hauled my suitcase into her trunk and let the door click shut.

Soon enough, someone behind us was honking impatiently. "I guess we'd better go," I said, looking anxiously at Bree. I gave Brian a quick squeeze, checked Avery's seatbelt one more time, then slid into the front seat and buckled up.

As we drove, we instantly fell into easy, flowing conversation. The girls, sitting backwards in their car seats, were babbling away, and from time-to-time even holding hands, as if they knew they had been destined to be best friends since birth.

It is a very strange sensation, meeting someone in person after you've met them online. I have always found it much easier to express myself through the written word, and I had been pouring out my soul online, in this place where I felt incredibly safe. We had been "internet friends" for over a year, but I swear we've been soul mates forever.

"This is wild. It seems totally unreal that you are in this car, sitting next to me," Bree said, giving my hand a squeeze. "I mean, think about this! You are in California! In LA! And you're coming to my new house to stay! We can go to Target together! And watch Teen Mom and Real Housewives of Orange County!!"

I laughed. "I seriously can't wait to just hang out with you. I don't even care that I'm in LA and we can't even really go anywhere. Except I might want to go to the grocery store and just stand there until we see a celebrity. Have you seen any lately?" We grinned.

Once we arrived at her house and unloaded my stuff, we set the girls down to play and sat on the couch, talking. "You know what the best thing about this is?" I asked. "The best thing is that I don't have to pretend anything about myself at all. Like, I don't have to pretend that I'm okay when I'm sad. And I can say to you, 'Hey, that sucks because dead babies,' and you totally get it. And you don't judge me for hating the pregnant bitches at Target even though you're not supposed to hate them (or anybody) at all. You're just like, 'oh, yeah, she looks like she's totally too perfect and probably mean.' Even though she doesn't really look mean. You just agree with me. And we know that we don't actually hate her, we are just sad and jealous, and we know that that will go away later, so we don't judge each other for that now, you know. I don't have to explain anything to you. You just get it. You know?"

Bree grinned. "I know! I do know exactly what you mean! It is just so easy and feels so awesome to be with you and talk to you. This is the best ever!"

Hours later, too many hours past our bedtime, I finally said, "Well, I guess we should call it a night, even though I totally don't want to."

Bree stared at me for a second. "I'm sure you're right, it's just that I *cannot believe* you are here! I feel like I don't want to waste a single hour that you're in town, even sleeping!" She put her hand on mine and tears began to stream down my face.

"This is so awkward," I said, "but I just need you to know that this is no little thing for me. You are my soul-sister, and I just cannot even imagine my life without you. Just . . . thank you. Thank you for everything."

Bree looked at me, her eyes welling up again with tears. After one more tight hug, still in total disbelief that we were so lucky, we finally agreed that it was time to hit the sack. After shutting my door and making sure Avery was still sleeping soundly, I dialed Brian. "Hey, babe!" I whispered. "You won't even believe how great today was . . ."

***

The next morning, we woke up early and started preparing for guests! Another blog friend of ours, Tina, who lived a few hours away, was willing to make the long trek to Bree's house to spend the day with us. Her husband was going to drive her around all the closed roads, which would tack on more than an hour to their trip.

I was nervous but excited. Everything felt so normal at Bree's—it was truly like we had known each other forever. I laughed, thinking about how I had told my friends that I was going to California to stay with a "friend from college." It was so ridiculous that I wasn't even "out" to my friends that I had met Bree online, yet here I was, in her house, helping her get ready for a little get-together.

When Tina and her sweet little Gigi walked in the door, my heart exploded. How strange it is when you finally meet these people you know about, you've seen pictures of, you've cried with, but never actually seen in person. Tina had lost twin girls, Sophia and Ellie, in a very similar way at a similar time as me. And Gigi, Nora, and Avery had been born within weeks of each other.

In the surreal magic of the moment, every smile, every laugh was evidence that together, we could heal. We were so lucky. The luckiest of the unlucky, we decided.

"How strange it is that the only people I actually feel comfortable with are people who, until today, I had never even met," I said.

Tina and Bree both nodded. "It's like people think the internet is fake and the people close to them are real, but it's sort of reversed for us," Bree added.

After Tina left and the girls were in bed, we coaxed Bree's husband into letting us leave for a while. We drove to the bottom of her street to the grocery store. Totally lame, right? Except to us, it was what we had been talking about for months. We walked slowly through the aisles, picking out snacks and discussing our day, gushing about how lovely Tina was. I imagined what it would be like to be able to do this whenever I wanted. To know that when I talked to someone, anything could be on the table to discuss, and my deepest, darkest, twistiest thoughts that came with my grief wouldn't be a shock.

Just when I thought it couldn't get any better, Bree got a text and told me we would be able to drive to our friend Rachel's house the next day. Rachel had lost triplets: Jaxon, Colin, and Courtney. I had found her blog online because she raised butterflies and would release them in your baby's name. From there, we hit it off, supporting each other throughout our stressful times.

We pulled up to a ranch-style house that looked perfectly Californian. As we got out of the car, excitement brewed in my stomach and my pulse quickened. We knocked on the door, but no one answered. Bree looked at me and then pushed the door open slowly. "Rach?"

We walked into the house and called for her again. "I'm out here!" we heard. We headed to the back of the house to see Rachel lying on the ground on her side with a pillow under her head. She was currently pregnant and had a small daughter, Kenzington. She was on strict bedrest due to a high-risk pregnancy, but she wanted to give her daughter some fresh air, so she was lying outside. We hugged crookedly, awkwardly, all of us, as tears streamed down our faces.

Rachel's backyard was one of the most beautiful places I had ever seen. Bright green grass, orange and lemon trees, a beautiful patio. The sun was shining down, and palm trees were sticking out over her fence. It was hot, but there was a breeze, and the blue skies blocked out any misery.

Our day was spent talking about baby stuff, pregnancy, and our losses. We vented to each other and listened without judging or giving unsolicited advice. Our stories were wildly different, but in the end they were the same. We were without our babies, but we had each other and these beautiful new lives to be wildly thankful for.

While we talked, all three of our baby girls waddled around

Rachel's beautiful yard, chasing butterflies and playing in the sandbox and enjoying the sun. Before we left, we were able to paint a butterfly on Rachel's garden wall in honor of our babies. I let Avery help me, and we painted two—one for Sophie and one for Aiden.

As we sat and visited in her backyard that day, Rachel was fighting so hard to get her baby son here safely, to give her daughter a sibling on earth. She does such an impressive job remembering her triplets, and she was one of the first people who made me feel like speaking my babies' names was NOT something annoying or bad. To be right there with her healed even more of my heart.

Recently, Rachel moved to a different state, and she had to paint over that wall of butterflies to sell her house. We all cried with her as she did this. It felt like the end of something, although like most things, it was also a new beginning.

That sense of belonging and the healing that comes with it cannot be underestimated. Yes, I had to fly across the country to get it, but I could practically feel my broken pieces starting to get glued back together. These women were my people; their babies felt like family to me. We were together in this, in the healing, and we were surviving.

***

Sitting on the airplane on the way back to Wisconsin, I felt sick to my stomach. It had been difficult when Bree dropped me off at the airport. I was going from this place of total ease back to where everything was hard. Back to where it felt like no one understood me at all, and I felt so judged. I was full of dread at the prospect of never seeing these ladies—my friends—again. They were no longer just names on comments.

I wonder all of the time how different my life would be if I had never gone to visit Bree. If I had been too weirded out or scared to go and stay at her house. These days, everyone in my life knows who

Bree *really* is. My best friend from the internet, not a friend from college who happened to move to LA. They know the story of how we met, and as far as I know, most of my people are cool with it. They think it's amazing, the bond we share. I have to say, I agree.

CHAPTER 16 - YOU'RE NOT GOING TO BELIEVE THIS

When Avery was about a year and a half old, I started wondering if I'd be able to give her a sibling. I had never planned to only have one child, but things had not exactly gone as I intended. The longing for the sweet baby smell and the feeling of a tiny babe falling asleep on my chest had been creeping in for a while, slowly nestling its way into my thoughts. My sister and I were seven years apart, and I wanted my children to be closer in age. So I knew that if I was going to do it, I needed to do it, and soon.

After Avery was born, though, I never went back on birth control. I think in the back of my mind, I kind of knew I wanted to have another baby, and with my fertility issues, it didn't make much sense for me to take hormonal birth control. And so for one and a half years we hadn't been using any kind of birth control at all. This just meant that a new baby would mean more money and more trips to the fertility clinic.

I also had sworn that I would lose a bunch of weight before I got pregnant again. I've tried to be thin since about fourth grade, though, and although I'm not the healthiest eater on the planet, I have always been active and tried to be more health conscious. But nothing really worked. My hormones were so wacky; to me, it was just another thing that was broken. Fifty pounds overweight? Add it to the list.

"Hey, Avery, do you want to have a little baby brother or sister?" I asked one day, while she played. Brian looked up from his laptop, a little twinkle in his eye.

"Are you serious?" he asked.

"I think so. I'm scared. And we'll need money, but I was thinking I should at least make the appointment now at the fertility clinic since they book so far out . . . that is, if you want to."

He grinned at me. That huge smile built my confidence. It would be difficult, but we could handle it! Later that day, I called and made an appointment with the same fertility specialist I had seen to get pregnant with Avery. I got the shivers, though, when I put down the phone. Was this really a good idea?

As the appointment approached, that shaky, uncertain feeling really began to creep its way in. The thought of doctor appointments, and questions, and blood sugar, and doctors without compassion clouded my mind; I couldn't even conjure up the image of a happy baby to take home in the end. I felt like I was tempting fate, like I was asking for too much. *How dare you, Christy? You got your one baby to raise. What makes you think you deserve more? Pressing your luck, aren't you?*

The day of my first appointment with Dr. Miller, my fertility doctor, went well. We'd stick with the same prescription that I had used before, a medication that would help my brain tell my body to ovulate. Then, a few weeks later, I'd have a transvaginal ultrasound, and we'd check how many mature follicles I had. We checked the number because if there were two pretty mature follicles on one side, we wouldn't try to get pregnant that month because the chance of conceiving twins was significantly higher.

This time felt so different than it did with both the twins and Avery. I just felt like I was going through the motions, almost expecting that it would not work. I had become pregnant on the first cycle with meds the last two times, so it would have been reasonable for me to hope for that, but I just didn't really feel that hope this time.

I also hardly told anyone that I was doing it. My life is a pretty open book, and people are used to me telling them everything (too much, really), but there was something holding me back. If I had to guess, it was me guarding myself because I didn't believe it would work this time.

The two weeks actually went by relatively quickly, and before I knew it, it was time for the ultrasound appointment to check for follicles. I had made the appointment for 7 a.m. so I could hopefully be done quickly and get to work before the students arrived. I went alone—Brian had to work, and he had taken Avery to daycare. It was winter in Wisconsin, though, and I left extra early because there was a pretty heavy snowfall, so even tried and true Wisconsinites would have to take it easy on the roads.

I trudged into the clinic, stomping the snow off of my shoes. As I waited in line to check in, my stomach started flip-flopping. A tall, thin nurse with kind eyes came out into the waiting room to take me back. "How are you today?" she asked.

"I'm good, thanks. Super excited to have a wand stuck up there, ya know," I said, with a laugh, feeling her out.

She giggled. "Right. Well, Dr. Miller isn't actually here this morning. She's running late because of the snow. So I'll send you in to get undressed from the waist down and sit up on the table with the blanket over your legs. Someone will be in as soon as they can."

Sitting naked from the waist down on a hard table with a paper blanket over your knees isn't as great as you'd think it is. However, there are much worse things, and after a certain point, you just don't care as much about what's going on down there. I sat at the edge of the table, looking around the dark room, checking my phone to watch the time. You can't exactly be late for work when you're an elementary school teacher. And Wisconsin schools don't know what snow days are!

Minutes later, a woman rushed into the room. She was short and stocky and had spiky hair that almost said, "Don't mess with me!" She didn't even look at me, she just snapped, "All right, let's get started, I don't have a lot of time," at the ultrasound tech, who moved very quickly to get the wand ready.

I tried not to cringe as the wand was inserted, and I reminded myself to relax, which is supposed to make it more "comfortable." She moved the wand around slowly, and I tried to see what she was seeing on the ultrasound screen.

The spiky-haired woman (Was she a doctor? I didn't even know.) stared at the screen, tapping her foot. "Okay, yep. So, you have one or two good-sized follicles in there. Just follow up with your doctor. I have to go."

I sat there, stunned. I was paying several hundred dollars for someone to "read" my ultrasound, and she tells me I have "one or two" follicles? Hello, that was the whole reason I was there! To know if it was one OR two. I gathered myself up and spoke, "Excuse me. But I need to know if there is one, or if there are two."

She whipped around and looked at me like I had three heads. "Look, I have my own patients. I don't have time for this. You have growing follicles like you should. I have to go."

Tears started rolling down my cheeks. The ultrasound tech was very quiet. Even in the dark, I could feel her discomfort.

"Are you kidding me right now? You're crying? I am a DOCTOR. I have OTHER PATIENTS."

I looked right at her, and I venomously choked out, "I had twins and they died. I'm trying not to have twins again. Did you even read my chart? I need to know if I should try to conceive this cycle or not."

"Maybe you don't understand how the female reproductive system works. I can see in the ultrasound that you have developing follicles and are getting ready to ovulate. I absolutely cannot tell you how many babies you would conceive if you tried right now. If I could do THAT, I would not be at this job."

The tears just kept flowing as the ultrasound tech handed me a towel and the doctor left the room. I didn't even know what had just happened. Was it me? Did I just have bad luck? Were most doctors just total assholes? Did I somehow deserve this, or bring it on myself?

"I'll have Dr. Miller call you," the tech said quietly. "I took a picture of the screen, and I'll put it in the notes to her so she can help you decide. I really hope you're okay."

I made my way back to school, crying the entire way. I was just shaken. Why had I thought I could do this? I wasn't ready. We weren't lucky. Our family wasn't ever going to be complete, so why would we bring this anxiety and pain on ourselves? By the time I got to school, I had decided. I was DONE. I simply refused to go down this road again.

By the time I saw Brian that night, he could tell something was up. I asked him to take care of Avery while I sat down and spent two hours typing up a letter to my hospital about the physician who had made me feel so awful. I then wrote a quick message to my actual fertility doctor and thanked her for her time, but told her I was on hold for treatment at this time. Before I sent either of them, I sat down and had Brian read them.

"So, you're sure this is what you want?" he asked, for the third time. "I mean, you don't have to see that doctor again. It'll be different the next time, when you can see Dr. Miller again. This isn't like you, to give up."

It didn't feel like giving up to me. It felt like taking control. I wanted it to be me saying, "I do not have to have this pain this time. I have a daughter who I need to care for. I am still grieving. I don't want to be treated like this." It was self-care. And sometimes it is absolutely necessary for our mommy hearts.

"I am going to focus on me," I told him. "I want to get serious about losing some weight and just take a step back. It's important that I make sure I stay mentally healthy, and this was not the way. I guess I just wasn't ready."

Brian nodded. I thought maybe I sensed disappointment in his eyes, but he didn't say anything. It was back to our normal, everyday life.

***

Two months later, I skipped into school, grinning. "You guys!" I yelled, and my coworkers slowly popped their heads out of their rooms. "Carolyn! Sarah! Come out here! You've got to see this!"

I led them outside the building and pulled a key fob from my pocket. "Get in!" I yelled. Running, we piled into my brand-new, white, fully-loaded Jeep. The ladies squealed. I turned the key, opened the sunroof, and blared the music. We drove around the block with the wind whipping through our hair, singing along to a song. *See,* I told myself, *I don't need another baby to be happy. I was just pressing my luck. It was a bad idea, anyway.*

And that new van that I loved so much? Screw it. I got rid of it. After Sophie and Aiden died, I hated that stupid thing with everything in me, for everything it represented. Naïve me, who thought that having a good twenty-week scan meant I would get to take two babies home. Miserable me for having to take the car seats out and drive the humongous thing around without any kids in it. Selfish me who was willing, for our family, to lose money on trading it in because I couldn't stand to be inside of it.

A few weeks later we were driving around our neighborhood in the new Jeep, visiting rummage sales. The sunroof was open and Avery was in the backseat, bouncing her little feet to the music. We drove around, the autumn breeze flowing through the car, as I listened to Brian talk about his day.

"So, then, she tells me that her mom owns her phone, not me, so if I want to take it from her, then her mom will sue me," he continued.

I looked over at him, and I wondered why he was breathing so . . . much. Why was he breathing so loudly? And would this story EVER end? I got it, the girl wanted to keep her phone. Ugh.

Avery kicked the back of my seat. "STOP IT!" I screamed.

"Woah," Brian said, raising his eyebrows at me.

I looked over at him and kinda wished I could punch him right in the face. He was SO annoying. I couldn't wait to get home so I didn't have to hear him scold me about whatever it was I wasn't doing right. And I wouldn't have to hear how LOUDLY he was breathing.

My cheeks flushed, and I leaned out my window to get some air. "I do NOT feel good, okay?" I mumbled.

As soon as we got home, I felt my cheeks flush red again, and a weird cramp down low. "Oh my gosh," I thought. This felt so . . . familiar: the moodiness, the nausea. But, there was no way. I ran upstairs to the bathroom, searching through my cupboard. Did I even have any pregnancy tests left?

I found one all the way in the back and sat down to take it. My heart was pounding. *Christy, you are so stupid. How many times have you convinced yourself you are pregnant, just to cry for a week about the negative pregnancy test? You CAN'T get pregnant on your own, you moron.*

Almost immediately, the hourglass stopped flipping and I looked down to see the word 'pregnant' staring back at me.

***

After I finished sobbing on the phone to Bree, I texted Dr. Brown.

> **You are not going to believe this.**

> **Um . . . you're pregnant?**

I made an appointment right away for a blood test, had my blood drawn, and a few days later I got THE call. "Hi, this is Mary from the clinic. We need you to come in because your progesterone is really low, too low for what we want to see. Can you come in tomorrow?"

I quickly Googled "low progesterone." Of course—it meant a high risk for miscarriage.

I knew it. A miscarriage. I was going to have a miscarriage.

At my appointment the next day, I got a prescription for progesterone supplements. They were vaginal suppositories that I had to use every night, and then I needed another blood test to see if my levels were rising. Every time I went to the bathroom, I checked the toilet paper, expecting to see blood.

A few weeks later, with my levels thankfully on the rise, I had an ultrasound to count the number of babies and to get a more precise due date. I walked into the ultrasound room at the clinic and was delighted to see it was the same tech who worked with that awful doctor.

She smiled at me as I got up on the exam table. A colleague of my doctor's came into the room to help me read the ultrasound. "So," she said. "I read your chart. We are hoping to see one baby on here today, I know. But, if we see two, I want you to remember to relax. We are going to do this, no matter what, okay? I also see we've had some scary progesterone levels. We'll make sure we think the size of the baby is matching up with how far along you think you are."

I felt so comforted by her words. The tech next to me had a little glimmer in her eyes, too. She was professional, but I could tell she wanted to comfort me. Brian held my hand as the tech zoomed in with her computer. "Well, I can only see one baby, so that is great news!" the doctor started. After taking a few measurements, she let us hear the heartbeat, and then the tech removed the wand and had me sit up.

"This baby looks great. You should keep taking the progesterone supplements until your body kicks in and starts making more of it on its own. This will probably happen around thirteen weeks. You just keep doing what you're doing." I let loose a sigh of relief. This wasn't over yet, but we had definitely crossed a hurdle.

***

As my pregnancy progressed, everyone, including me, really expected things to get easier. After all, I had somehow managed to get Avery here in perfect health, so what was the problem?

I got the question so often: "So, it's easier this time, right? Since it worked with Avery?" more times than I could count. I started lying in my reply, managing a "Yep, it's better, thanks." But, truthfully, my anxiety was just as bad.

This pregnancy was not easy, from the very beginning to the very end. I had gestational diabetes again, and so I had to have non-stress tests every week once I got to thirty weeks. Those tests ironically made my anxiety (and my blood pressure) skyrocket like crazy. I felt like a terrible mom to Avery, terrified to lift her into her car seat, frozen with fear if she accidentally ran into my belly or kicked me. I was short with her and irritable.

After one of my non-stress tests that I almost didn't pass, I was lying in bed next to Brian and couldn't shut off my mind. It was dark in our bedroom except for a little flash of light blinking on the humidifier that was making tiny bubbling sounds. I lay there, thinking, wondering if

Brian was awake and thinking, too. "Hey, babe?" I asked, quietly.

"Yeah?"

"I can't ever do this again." My mouth tasted dry, metallic as I tried to say the words I had rolled over in my mind again and again.

"Do what again?" he asked, sitting up a little.

"Be pregnant. Have another baby."

He laughed. "Just the thought of managing Avery *and* this little guy making you nervous?"

I sat up and looked at him. "I can't be pregnant again. I know I will probably want more children someday, but I can't do it. If this baby lives, I don't ever want to do this again."

"Okay," Brian said. Not slowly, not annoyed, not sharp, just, "okay."

Well, that's that.

"Okay," I said, finally ready to fall asleep.

***

Evan James Wopat was born on December 31, 2012, at 9:48 in the morning. He is a constant source of joy for me, and I'm so lucky I was able to give Avery a sibling to play with—and fight with, of course! He has allowed me to experience the joy (and fear) of raising a boy, and he has probably taken a few years off of my life with his uninhibited bravery and stubborn attitude.

He was born via planned repeat C-Section, and I also had a tubal ligation. Now, almost every day I wish I hadn't had it, but I'm also glad I did. I am so grateful for months spent never wondering if my period is late or just isn't coming for a few months. I'm so thankful that I will never have to wonder if a baby will die inside of me, or come out too early, or if something I eat will cause it to be sick or stillborn.

When I see families with three children, my heart hurts. *I should have waited,* I think. *Three is the perfect number. We should have had three.* But, honestly, somewhere deep down I know that if I had had three, I would think we should have four. I really don't know what it's like for "regular" families to decide when they are "done," but I think I will never really feel like my family is complete, no matter how many children we had here with us. I could spend forever trying to fill that void. No matter how hard I try, though, it can never be. I am grateful for my little family, and Sophie and Aiden will always be gone, but they will also always be a piece of our family's puzzle.

CHAPTER 17 - FIND YOURSELF A BREE

This morning at breakfast, in between shoving heaping spoonfuls of cereal into his mouth, Evan asked me, "Mama? Have I always lived in this house?"

"Yep," I replied. "And so has your sister. Well, we moved here from our other house when I was pregnant with her. When she was still in my belly."

He thought that over for a second and then asked, "Well, why did we move to this house?"

There's always a decision I have to make when I'm answering my kids. My students, too. One thing I feel strongly about is that whenever you *can* be honest and it's developmentally appropriate, I think you should.

So, I took a deep breath, and I answered, "We moved here because the other house made me sad."

From across the table, Avery chimed in. "She means she was sad because of Sophie and Aiden."

Evan looked right at me. "Mama? They died, right?"

"Yes, honey, they did."

Without missing a beat, he put his little, chubby hand on my arm and asked, "Mama? Why do babies die?"

Think, Christy. How do you answer this? How do you tell your baby boy that you have no idea why? That there are things in this world that you will never understand?

Before I could answer, Avery said matter-of-factly, "You know, Evan. If they hadn't died, we wouldn't be here. Right, Mom? We wouldn't be alive if they were."

I can tell you with complete certainty that I have NEVER said this or anything like this to her. So, how does a six-year-old brain come to this conclusion?

It's not like I haven't thought about this before. It's not even like people haven't said this to me before in an attempt to make me feel better. ("Well, you know, you wouldn't have that darling Avery, and she's pretty special!") But there really is no way to reconcile this in my mind. It's in a place that is so far back that I just cannot actually access it without causing major damage.

Have you ever played a game called "Scruples?" Some of the questions are easy for me to answer: Yes, I would give the money back. No, I wouldn't steal that if I had the chance. Of my four limbs,

I'd rather give my left arm. Of all five senses, I'd rather give up my sense of sound so I don't have to hear all of your shitty attempts to pacify me. But a question like, "If you could go back in time and change it so that you never lost the twins, would you do it?"

Rolling that question over in my mind is torture. It's a question that I know, gratefully, I don't ever have to answer. Life is so messy, and so complicated, and it is full of things to contemplate. That's part of the beauty of it all, right?

My living children will always know about Sophie and Aiden. We'll all remember them together, for as long as we can. And the best part is, although it took a while, I know I don't have to do it alone. I have my family, and my friends, and even strangers who understand tragic loss. I am not the same person I used to be, that is for sure. I've come to realize, however, that there is nothing I can do about that. All I can do is keep working on the person I have become and trust in the person who I will be. But no matter the past, the present, or the future . . . I am a mother.

***

If you looked at my family today, without knowing our story, you'd probably think it was on the "too good to be true" side of the spectrum as far as family happiness and picture perfect images go: two children, one boy and one girl, at a perfectly-spaced, "must have been planned out," two and a half years apart. My husband and I are both respected teachers in great school districts. We have a lovely house and get to go on vacations . . . when I can stop spending so much money on Amazon and save enough.

If you didn't look closely, you would never know that I struggled with fertility. You might not know that I take anti-anxiety medication because I never could quite get those thoughts about everybody dying out of my head. You probably wouldn't know that my blood pressure goes up every time I walk into a doctor's office, even when the appointment isn't for me.

You wouldn't be able to see that Brian still pictures the moment his dad died, and that because of it, he can't watch any TV shows that are bloody because it gives him nightmares. Or that on his key ring he carries a scuffed up, barely legible keychain that I gave him for his first Father's Day, when the children he was supposed to be a father to weren't anywhere to be seen, except in tiny urns. You wouldn't know that he still carries so much guilt that he couldn't do anything more to stop them from dying.

We, as human beings, we carry so much. We have these invisible weights on our shoulders, pushing us down. And we sometimes think that we are the only ones. We weather it alone because we don't want to seem fragile or weak. For the longest time, I held it all in. I did what everyone else did and posted perfect, filtered photos of everyone smiling. The four of us, grinning, on our perfect train ride. What a magical, beautiful thing to do with your family. Of course you couldn't see in the picture that I was crying, that the tears come every single time we do something special. With every joy for me, there will always be longing.

The more I share, the more honest I am, the more real I get, the more I hear from people that they are so grateful for just that. That they are so moved by my honest and raw account of my journey with grief that it has helped them along in their own. And the thing is, I am not doing anything special. Honesty is not *really* all that special. Sure, it makes me vulnerable, but I've learned that being vulnerable isn't such a bad thing after all.

***

Last summer, I texted Bree:

Hey. B and I are coming to Vegas for
our 10th. You meeting us there?

OMG. Yes. Do you want to see Britney? Ooh,
or Michael Jackson Cirque? What dates are
you going? Let me see if I can make it work!

Brian and I had the best time in Vegas. We stayed in a hotel way nicer than one we could actually afford. We wandered through casinos and held hands and ate delicious dinners. And, of course, we talked about our kids. All of them. Sophie and Aiden will always be a part of our conversation. Even though they're not in the forefront like, "Seriously, did you see what Avery made in art at school the other day?" they are always in the picture.

We wonder who they would have been. What their personalities would have been like. Which of us they would have looked liked. We talk about how insane it would be to have all four of them here with us. Recently, a good friend of mine surprised me by stopping by our house with a gift.

"I hope you like this," she said. "It's a little scary to give it to you because I don't want to hurt you."

I opened it cautiously. Inside was a beautiful framed drawing of all four of my children, together in one photo. Needless to say, it is one of my most prized possessions. It reminds me that our loss is a part of our story, and that means forever.

In the beginning, I loathed the question, "Do you have any children?" I would labor over my answer, pausing, waiting for my cheeks to stop burning. A battle would ensue inside my brain. I'd analyze the person, trying to determine how they would react if I told the truth. Mentally, I'd practice. "I have two kids in Heaven, none on Earth." Or, "I had two babies, but they died." Or, "None that are living." Then, inevitably, something less practiced or polished would slip out, or I'd simply answer, "Nope." Of course, whenever I said no, I would privately lash myself for not honoring the twins' memory, or for lying, or just in general not doing the right thing.

It's been some time since I've done that. I now say, "Two," referencing the two living children that I have. I suppose once I became a mom to living children I didn't feel the need to fight so hard. I could say two, be deemed a mother, and then move on. Also, in general I actually try diligently *not* to meet new people so that I don't have to explain anything at all. I know that is pathetic, but it's true.

On our second day in Las Vegas, we got picked up at our hotel in a cheesy 1980s limousine and taken to a little white wedding chapel off the strip to renew our vows. My husband is super awesome, and he agreed for us to have the ceremony in Elvis's pink Cadillac in the "Tunnel of Love."

We arrived wearing our cheesy "Still Rockin' and Rollin' after 10 years!" T-shirts (mine white and his black). Right before the ceremony started, the officiant asked me if we had kids and how many. I'm not exactly sure why, but I replied, "Yes, we have four."

"Wow!" she chirped. "You must have your hands full! Four kids!"

She continued, "The two of you have created four beautiful children, and now you have your hands full every day and night. Four little people under your feet, and you hardly have any time to yourselves, to pay attention to your marriage. With four children here needing you, you really have to carve out time to devote to each other . . ."

That familiar feeling of grief worked its way in and around. I eyed up the exits, looking for a getaway. I wanted this to be silly and cheesy and fun, and instead I sat there, frozen, wondering how I could correct her, or get her to stop, or go back in time and just say "two." On the other hand, my mind wandered to what it would really be like to have all four of my children here.

I have yet to be able to watch the video recording of the ceremony that I paid way too much money for. It's hard for me to believe that after all these years, I still struggle with this. That after all these years, I haven't made a firm decision about what I'll say or do, and that it still affects me. I guess there's never really an end.

***

On my desk at work, I have a small green ceramic figurine of four peas in a pod. Each morning, as I dump all of my bags down on my chair, I always notice the figurine. All of the peas are smiling, like they are nothing but content to be together. And each morning, when I notice the smiling peas, I whisper Sophie and Aiden's names into the universe again.

Every so often, a student will be talking to me while I'm at my desk and they'll point to the figurine. "Is that because your whole family is like four peas in a pod?" I'm the kind of teacher who is very transparent and upfront with my students, and so I tell them, "Those are for all four of my children, and depending on the day that makes me feel peace or pain."

When we experience great loss, we experience complex emotions that make us feel subhuman. It does not feel great to feel what might be actual hatred toward a woman you have never met simply because she is pregnant and walking around Target. It doesn't feel good to not be able to have a normal conversation at lunch in the teachers' lounge because everything everybody says just hurts too much.

It makes you feel ashamed and lonely and wonder what's wrong with you. But, in the end, there's nothing wrong with you at all. It's normal for that grief to twist you and make you angry, sad, and lost. It makes us jealous and full of rage and desperation and weepiness and despair. We want to scream to the world, "DOESN'T ANYONE

UNDERSTAND THAT THIS IS NOT FAIR?!" And that, really, is because it's not fair. Nothing really is. But we have to be careful because if we start asking why these *horrible* things happened to us, we'd also have to ask why these other *great* things happened to us. Really, the truth is, there's just no point in asking.

Eventually, you arrive at a point where you realize that everyone is carrying some sort of heavy burden around. And we could all argue that what we are carrying around is somehow "worse." But it's not worth it. We need to try to understand, stop using clichés, and just really *listen to each other*. Ask your friend or loved one what the worst part is. What they are most afraid of. What they can't get out of their minds. Try not to be annoyed when they've said the same thing five hundred times, and it seems like they *just can't move on*. Or at least, don't let it show that you are!

As I've mentioned, my life is divided into two parts: before the twins and after the twins. And while I thought I was an empathetic person before, the truth is, I wasn't. Not really. I was caring and compassionate, but I think true empathy might only be realized once you have needed someone else's empathy to survive the day.

The love and kindness that my blog friends gave me saved my life. I do not even really have the words to thank my ladies for everything that they did for me. I don't know if Avery and Evan would be here if it weren't for their support. I wrote out all my fears, and they nodded and said, "Uh huh, yes, yep. Those are my fears, too. But you've got this. You can do it." And, most of us got it. Most of us got to be mamas to babies who we get to love and hug and raise.

Literal strangers, women who live in Texas and California and Vermont and Missouri and Australia and England—these women raised *me* up. They let me know in no uncertain terms that they would read my words, and they wouldn't try to give me advice. Instead, they would just tell me that they were sorry I was hurting. That they knew how awful it was, and that they wished it didn't have to be that way.

"I wish that Sophie and Aiden were here with you now."

Those words. They both comforted and stung. That had been all I ever wanted. And it was all I would never have.

***

On our last night in Las Vegas, Bree and her husband arrived. We went out to a fancy dinner and a show. We had champagne and walked down the strip and the husbands got to know each other better while Bree and I walked side by side and giggled.

As the night turned into early morning, and we started thinking about our early flight the next day, Bree and I looked at each other and grinned. "How FUN is this?" I laughed. It was SO strange to be together, in such a different place, having so much fun.

"Hey," Bree said. "We had to live through the pain together; we totally deserve to get to have some fun together, too!"

She was right. That night in Las Vegas, with my kids cared for and safe at home, celebrating the fact that Brian and I had made it through ten years of marriage, having Bree and her husband go to so much trouble just to see us . . . I was on top of the world! I felt a sense of peace that was almost inexplicable. If you are reading this and you have just experienced a loss, this is my promise to you. This will not be easy; it will take so much work. The pain will feel insurmountable some days, and you will want to give up. But if you work at your grief, if you chip away at it, if you allow yourself to know that grief will redefine you and change you as a person, you are going to be okay.

Our friends and family members who have not lived through terrible grief have these unrealistic expectations about time. In my experience, after a year is up, people think you are supposed to be done. Absolutely done. They say things like, "It's been a year, what could still be wrong with you? Doesn't time heal all wounds?" They look at the calendar and decide, "Oh, she should be good now! Why isn't she happier? It's been long enough!"

Time won't heal you, but your hard work will. Tell your friends and family what you need. If they can't give it to you, it's up to you to find people who will. Go find yourself a Bree! There is somebody out there who is going through the same kinds of pain that you are right now. Someone is sitting at their computer, Googling, "What do I do when my baby dies?"

The world is this huge place full of amazing people who have so much to offer you, and you don't have to be alone. Find one and be one. Remember: We've got this.

Text exchange between Bree and Christy, circa 2013:

> somebody should seriously write a book using all our crazy txts to each other

> u should do it! It'll be a best seller!

> I can see it now! We'll call it "When u think ur crazy but it turns out everyone else is too!" and in it we can make sure that we remember the twins and Ella.

> and we can include the story of how you came all the way out here to LA thinking I might be a 60 yr old man

> LOL. Could we really do it? We could write about Ella, and Sophie, and Aiden, and now my Avery and Evan, and your Nora and Isla. We could write about how we found each other and just about the whole thing. It could be a book about us!

> OMG. A book about us. Love it!

CHAPTER 18 - ALMOST A MOTHER

*Photo courtesy of Apropos Photography

Almost a Mother
As Told in *Listen to Your Mother*, a Production by Ann Imig

There was a time when my motherhood was invisible. I did have some tangible pieces of evidence. Two tiny urns—one blue, one pink. A white note card with four smudged footprints, and hospital bills piled on the counter. Two matching cribs, lying in pieces, hidden underneath a sheet in the garage.

I walked around, my motherhood invisible, while grief waged an all-out war on my attitude. Pregnant bellies caused an eye roll and a huff while double strollers induced a raging tantrum. A pregnancy announcement would cause a night of tears, my husband holding my hand, desperate to help. I sat through stories at lunch about first steps and first words. *Really?* I'd think. *My babies are still dead.*

I was still in the hospital when the first relative tried to comfort me. "Hey, you'll have more kids," she said. "And besides, those two definitely had something wrong with them, or God would have saved them. They probably would have been serial killers."

I wish I were making that up.

I wanted to scream the words. "I had two babies! I am still their mom! Can't you see?" That failed, and so I whispered, "I had two babies . . ." But when I whispered, people still looked away. They shuddered. "Don't talk about it," their eyes commanded. Shrugged shoulders and tilted heads told me what I already knew: "Move on. We already have."

For months I tried to move on. "What are you even so upset about?" I'd ask myself. "They lived for like a day. You didn't even hold them until they were dying, and then that was it." So all the nursery furniture went up on Craigslist, and out it went. Memories were shoved in a box. Reminders would make it worse.

My heart insisted, "But they were your children! She wrapped her whole hand around your finger. You carried them for months. It was only your voice they knew. You can't just move on! Their memory is yours to keep alive!"

It went on that way for a while, the back and forth. And then, it was Mother's Day. We were headed to a family cookout. Surely, everyone would remember I'm a mother.

Instead, we arrived and instantly the averted eyes and silence told me this day was not meant to celebrate me. "You're a fool," I scolded myself. "You should have known better."

Later that day, I found myself out shopping with my mom and my six-year-old nephew. I tossed my items on the conveyor belt so that they'd get charged to my mom, and I ducked out of the way, grinning. The clerk looked up as she scanned. "Hey," she said. "Isn't today Mother's Day? Shouldn't you be buying this stuff for her?"

"Oh, that's my daughter for ya," my mom laughed.

The clerk laughed, too. "I hope *you* remember that someday when you are a mother."

I sucked in a breath.

My nephew piped up from behind me, "Aunt Christy was almost a mother," he told her. "But then she wasn't anymore."

I turned and ran out of the store, the tears burning in the corners of my eyes. I made it to the parking lot, but then my sobs became uncontrollable.

"What's the matter, Aunt Christy?" my nephew asked.

"Oh, nothing, buddy," I choked out. "I'm okay."

I got into the back of the car, feeling the grief work its way in and around, curling itself into me like tendrils of smoke. Silence surrounded me once again.

I went home that night, and I started a blog, which I titled "Almost a Mother." The very first line read, "Contrary to the title of this blog, I *am* a mother." I spent night after night writing our story. Writing while I was crying so hard that I could barely see the screen. Writing through anger that made me feel insane. Writing through my next two pregnancies that were fraught with anxiety and straight-up terror.

Today, my motherhood is more apparent to the people around me. They can easily see Avery and Evan, my six and four-year-olds. I try to be honest about the fact that motherhood is amazing, like when your kid is star of the week and all they want is for *you* to have lunch with them, and how sometimes it is *not* amazing, like when they throw up all over your bathroom counter, or when they break your TV by "surfing" on the TV stand while you're cooking dinner.

But, I won't let the *other* part of my motherhood be invisible. So, I continue to say their names. Sophie and Aiden. They are my children, too. I will honor their memory forever, in any way that I can. I truly do not know who I would be if this hadn't happened to us.

In the end, I know that my sweet nephew had NO idea that his words would carry such meaning. He was looking at it in the most black-and-white, six-year-old kind of way. But he was just saying out loud what everyone else was thinking. I am forever grateful that he did say those words, though, because they made me realize that I was not ALMOST a mother. I AM a mother.

ACKNOWLEDGMENTS

First and foremost, I need to thank my husband, Brian, for his unwavering support. He never once doubted the fact that I could write an entire book while teaching full time and raising two small children. He believed in me more than I believed in me. He also wrangled the kids while I worked on this for hours at a time and did it all while knowing this project could end up being read only by me. He also stood by my side during the darkest hours of my life, and instead of running away, he held me close. I love you.

Avery and Evan, you absolutely saved my life. I love you so much that I can't stand it. You are both smart and hilarious and stubborn, and you make my whole life worth living.

To Orange Hat Publishing, THANK YOU for taking a chance on me. I'm forever grateful. Shannon, you are the best!

To Chrissy, my editor, I honestly don't know how I got so lucky to work with you. From the first email that you wrote to me, I knew you were FANTASTIC and that we fit together so well! It's too bad Shannon didn't let us pick the title we *really* wanted!

To my editor, friend, and colleague Alyssa Harlan, who read every sentence in every chapter, and who sat with me for hours trying to come up with titles and business plans, and who gave me more encouragement than I ever deserved—thank you. I'm so lucky to have you in my life!

Thank you to Sarah St. John and Julia Vail, who told me from the very beginning that I just needed to get my story out. Thank you for being there every single step of the way, through all the bad and all the good. It means the world.

I owe so much to my little writer's critique group, Pete and Kelly. You both gave me so much hope and encouragement and joy. You helped me get my story out and find my voice. You took me seriously, and you were brave enough to critique me when a lot of people couldn't or wouldn't. You both mean so much to me. Thank you.

Thank you Heather, Carolyn, Jess, Jen, Kate, Chuck & Becky, Crystal, Stacie, Tracy, Kari, Laura, Anne, and Katie for your comments and suggestions, and for reading and rereading my words to help me improve. You rock!

To my friends and family, you have never questioned my truth or my need to share this so honestly, and you have tried so hard to support me in whatever way you could manage. I know it's been hard. I love you all.

I can't even believe I get to write this, but thank you to Colleen Hoover, New York Times Best Selling Author, who treated me like I was SOMEBODY and showed me that there is still goodness in the world. Go buy all her books. Right now.

To my online sisters, thank you for helping me learn to live again. Thank you for being there when I had no one else. You made me realize that none of us ever have to be alone.

And finally, to Bree, my soul sister and my lifeline—thank you! I love you, always and forever.

See you in Vegas! xo

Resources

http://stillstandingmag.com/
An online magazine dedicated to giving a voice to grief

http://www.grieveoutloud.org/
A resource that provides ways to help families find their way back to
life after pregnancy and infant loss.

https://www.nowilaymedowntosleep.org/
A non-profit organization that provides beautiful remembrance
photography.

https://www.compassionatefriends.org/
Supports grieving families.

http://facesofloss.com/
This site provides stories of loss and stories of hope, reminding
bereaved families that they are not alone.

ABOUT THE AUTHOR

Christy Wopat, a fourth-grade teacher, and her husband, Brian, are raising two adorable children ages 5 and 7 in Holmen, WI. But Christy has two other children—twins—who died shortly after being born at 24 weeks.

She began writing as a way to process through her grief and never stopped. She currently contributes to several online magazines as well as a podcast, hoping to help raise awareness about pregnancy and infant loss.

www.christywopat.com

Made in the USA
Monee, IL
16 June 2020